KEEP CHOOSING yes

BECKY SPAHR

Following Jesus beyond the
confines of your comfort zone

Copyright © 2021 by Becky Spahr
All rights reserved.
978-0-578-95638-1

Cover design and illustration by Becky Spahr.

Unless otherwise indicated, all Scripture quotations are from The ESV® Bible (The Holy Bible, English Standard Version®), copyright © 2001 by Crossway, a publishing ministry of Good News Publishers. Used by permission. All rights reserved.

Scripture quotations marked (NLT) are taken from the Holy Bible, New Living Translation, copyright ©1996, 2004, 2015 by Tyndale House Foundation. Used by permission of Tyndale House Publishers, Carol Stream, Illinois 60188. All rights reserved.

Scripture quotations marked (NIV) are taken from the Holy Bible, New International Version®, NIV®. Copyright © 1973, 1978, 1984, 2011 by Biblica, Inc.™ Used by permission of Zondervan. All rights reserved worldwide.

Scripture quotations marked (MSG) are taken from THE MESSAGE, copyright © 1993, 2002, 2018 by Eugene H. Peterson. Used by permission of NavPress, represented by Tyndale House Publishers. All rights reserved.

Jess –
Thanks for always encouraging me to say yes.
For being there for me in the dark.
For putting my hand in the hand of Jesus.
Love you, friend.

table of contents

Dear Friend ---------- 11

01 – Yes to Saying Yes ---------- 13

02 – Yes to Restoration ---------- 21

03 – Yes to Discomfort ---------- 29

04 – Yes to Losing Myself ---------- 37

05 – Yes to the Mission ---------- 45

06 – Yes to the Lonely Places ---------- 55

07 – Yes to Surrender ---------- 63

08 – Yes to Asking for Help ---------- 71

09 – Yes to Staying ---------- 79

10 – Yes to Being Uprooted ---------- 89

11 – Yes to Dying ---------- 97

12 – Yes in the Darkness ---------- 105

The Space Between ---------- 114

13 – Yes When I'm Afraid ---------- 115

14 – Yes to Eye Contact ---------- 125

15 – Yes to Standing Firm ---------- 135

16 – Yes to Coming Close ---------- 143

17 – Yes to Coming to Know --------------------------------------- 153

18 – Yes to Peace --- 161

19 – Yes to the Hard Work --- 169

20 – Yes to Abiding --- 177

21 – Yes to What's Next --- 183

P.S. Still Choosing Yes --- 189

Thank You --- 191

Notes --- 193

Psalm 66:16

"Come and hear, all you who fear God,
and I will tell what he has done for my soul."

Dear Friend,

From the bottom of my heart, thank you for picking up this book. It means a lot to me; really, it does.

This book, *my first book* (and hopefully not my last!), was birthed out of a season of struggle. A season of wrestling and spinning in seemingly endless circles. A long stretch of darkness met with lots of loneliness. There were times of doubt, times I wanted to quit. But something, or rather, Someone, hasn't let me give up hope.

I am a Jesus follower. And in the last four years, it is as if my eyes have been opened to what I "signed up for" just over two decades ago when I said yes to Jesus for the first time. Following Jesus isn't always easy, it isn't always fun, and it often isn't very comfortable.

But is it worth it?

Last year, I felt like I came to a point in my life where God was asking me to choose. Was he worth it? Was I all in? Or was it all a façade? Did my heart really belong to Jesus? Or was I trying to serve two masters?

What if I told you right now that you had to make a choice between Jesus and comfort? My lips have always been quick to say his name, but my heart has moved a little slower. I believe we are faced with this exact decision every single day in some way or another, and I also believe that most of the time, many of us choose comfort. I know that some days I still do.

What I am learning, though, is that just as exercising is pretty hard to do from the couch, following Jesus is pretty hard to do from within the confines of our comfort zones. The word "following" in and of itself implies movement of some sort, and hopefully, movement *forward*. To be a follower implies you've pledged your allegiance to a leader, and that leader is, well, *leading* you somewhere. It's a simple concept, really; so simple we've made it into a child's game. But are you actually following? Are you actually moving behind the leader? *Wherever* he goes?

These next pages hold parts of my story as a follower, the lessons I've learned along the way, and the things into which God has graciously invited me. These pages also hold an invitation for you: to get off the couch, to say yes to following Jesus, and to ***keep* choosing yes**.

Much love,

Becky

01

yes to saying yes

You and I are constantly being told to learn how to say the word "no." *Set boundaries*, they say. *Self-care comes before everything and everyone*, the ads on social media scream. *Self-protect*, the world shouts. Don't be a people pleaser; cut toxic people out of your life. Do whatever you need to do to ensure your own happiness. Self-help, self-improve! Take selfies! Self, self, self!

I got the word "no" down pretty early in life, much thanks to my D.A.R.E. officer (say no to drugs!) and my mom. I have more than one memory of her reading scenarios from the book *Sticky Situations* at the breakfast table to my brother and me, posing a hypothetical moral dilemma and discussing how we ought to respond. And although I was never, not even once, offered drugs in the school yard (a rite of passage I was sure that every middle schooler would encounter at one point or another), I am not being facetious when I say that those early morning chats helped shape me as a young woman who knows how to stand her ground.

I have undoubtedly benefited greatly from growing in my ability to stand firm, set healthy boundaries, and say no to *over*-scheduling myself, especially as someone who leans towards wanting to please everyone, and yet I am beginning to see how the common mentality of being quick to say no has in some ways stunted my growth as a Jesus-follower. And I don't think I'm alone in that. I understand, support, and value the importance of learning how to say no; yet, simultaneously, I fear that we're becoming a generation of women and men who have forgotten how to say *yes*.

Let me be clear: I do not endorse saying yes to drugs, peer pressure, abusive relationships, or anything else along those lines. And for those struggling with mental health, setting very clear and strict boundaries is of utter importance. Please, continue to teach your children, and yourselves, how to say no; this was such a valuable lesson my mother taught me. But in a world that delivers messages straight to our inboxes telling us that everything revolves around self-care, self-improvement, and self-love, perhaps some of us have forgotten how to be selfless. And oftentimes, saying yes requires selflessness, while saying no comes from a place of selfishness.

I know firsthand that yes isn't always easy. It isn't always comfortable. Yes can make us feel weary and tired. Yes means saying no to other things, and maybe something better will come along later. Yes stretches our limits. But yes is also the anthem of a willing servant. Yes is the indication of obedience and submission to authority. Yes tells your friends and family that you care about them. Yes is a song of hope to the ears of those who have heard only no. And, for me, as a disciple of Jesus, yes is the only proper response to the invitations extended from the One who laid down his life on my behalf.

* * *

I said yes to Jesus for the first time when I was a mere six years old. I was at Wednesday night church, and I prayed a sweet and honest silent prayer, "inviting him into my heart." Those are the words I used then, but now I know that it was Jesus who invited *me* to come close to *his* heart.

That night, at age six, was the night I was saved. The night I became a Christian and started a relationship with Jesus. The night I first took on my identity as a believer. I'm starting to see, though, that there is a difference between being a believer and being a follower, a difference between being saved and being a disciple. Our salvation takes but an instant; our discipleship, or as some call it, "apprenticeship" to Jesus, takes a lifetime.

Many of us, including myself, initially failed to realize that the invitation to believe would be only the first of many throughout our lives as Jesus-followers. We said the first yes, but sooner or later we found ourselves a comfortable spot to settle into. We developed a routine, and we started to forget that the invitation was not to stay in the same place with Jesus, but to *follow* him. And we do have a choice; we can say yes, or we can say no. But as much as we might want it to be so, there's no grey area on this matter.

Can I ask you a hard question? What is your response when God extends a new invitation? An invitation to move, to quit your job, to share the gospel with a stranger? An invitation to break up with your girlfriend or boyfriend, to write a book, to ask someone for forgiveness? To lead a small group, to go back to school, to downsize your house and your lifestyle? What happens when God asks you to do something outside of your comfort zone? Something that sounds crazy? Something you really do not want to do?

Is your first instinct to say no?

Have you become so content with your spot on the couch or in the pews that you have no momentum to move forward?

Have you become so conditioned by the world to say no to things that don't make you happy or comfortable, that you wouldn't give a second thought to saying no to God?

Read those questions again, out loud maybe, and sit with them for a minute.

* * *

Over the last four years, I've been presented with many invitations from God that I've really wanted to say no to. I tried to say no, believe me. On more than one occasion, saying no has been my first instinct, the first word out of my mouth. But God has graciously poked me a little harder, asked me a little louder. And he's so patient with me. He's asked me to say some really hard yeses that have required me to step pretty far outside my comfort zone. I've had to choose to be obedient to God many times over my own personal preference. I've had to remind myself to submit to his will rather than my own. I've had to keep choosing yes.

I won't sugarcoat it; it's been hard. Really hard. But let me tell you, friend: obedience is always worth it. Because doing something that Jesus wants you to do, even when uncomfortable, is always better than living a life outside his will. Following Jesus is *worth it*. I've experienced times of loneliness and heartbreak and fear and anxiety and discomfort, yes. But I've also been given overwhelming peace and extreme joy and friendship with Jesus and opportunities I could have never imagined.

We live in a culture that tells us we should make our decisions based on what *feels good* to us. That our feelings dictate our own personal truths. That we can base our whole lives and belief system on our feelings. Unfortunately, I don't think our feelings are always accurate reflections of truth, and I don't think Jesus' call was to follow him only if we feel like it. Following Jesus when it didn't *feel* good has been good *for* me. My dependence on Jesus has increased, as has my fruit-bearing capacity. I'm flourishing in ways I didn't expect. And the more I say yes, the easier the next yes becomes.

* * *

Like I said earlier, I've been a Christian most of my life, but only in recent years have I begun to understand Jesus' invitation to come and follow him, *really* follow him. It's been an ongoing journey of learning to keep moving forward even when I want to turn around. To keep faithfully putting one foot in front of the other in pursuit of following Jesus. Learning to say yes even when it's downright painful. Being willing to stay even when I want to run.

I was never into sports or athletics, so it's come as a shock to many, but I've been running a lot lately (for exercise, not from my problems…okay, from my problems, too). I'm not competitive, I'm not really an athlete, and I give up way too easily. I'd rather sit on the grass in the sun all day and listen to music or a podcast. But for some reason, only by the divine intervention of Jesus himself I am sure, I'm into it. I like to go out on the country roads between all the fields and farms and run and run in a straight line, eyes fixed in one spot until I reach it; and then I pick a new target to focus on and keep going. It's teaching me about endurance. How to keep going even when it's really hard. I have to just keep putting one foot in front of the other, knowing eventually I'll reach the end…that with every step, I'm getting closer.

Running is a lot like life with Jesus. It's challenging and (literally) breathtaking at times, but you also have moments of relief and moments of victory, and sometimes you just hit that stride and you're cruising along like an Olympic athlete! And sometimes you stumble on a tiny little rock, or maybe a big one, and you lie on the side of the road for a while. But you should always get back up, because—spoiler alert—if you're running with Jesus, he always wins.

This book is my encouragement to keep running. To say no to quitting early, and yes to perseverance. To say no to becoming complacent and sitting on the couch all day, and yes to getting out there and running after Jesus. I love the way Eugene Peterson interprets Apostle Paul's message in 1 Corinthians 9:26-27 (MSG): "I don't know about you, but I'm running hard for the finish line. I'm giving it everything I've got. No sloppy living for me! I'm staying alert and in top condition. I'm not going to get caught napping, telling everyone else all about it and then missing out myself."

Let's run hard for the finish line, friends! If you said yes to Jesus' first invitation but you aren't willing to say yes to the ones to come, *what was the point of even starting the race?*

* * *

Maybe you've been lying on the side of the road for a while. Maybe you've slowed down to a walk or a crawl. Maybe you've straight up left the track, gotten in your car, and driven home to lie on your couch and eat potato chips. Or maybe you've been running for a while now, and you're really hitting that stride. I don't know where you're at in the race, but what I do know is that it's never too late to start running again. And I don't think Jesus is on the sidelines screaming at you with a stopwatch. He's the one with a foam finger and a huge sign that reads, "KEEP GOING!"

Unfortunately for those of us who lean a little bit towards laziness (I'm talking to myself right now), his sign does *not* say,

"RUNNING IS EASY!" or "THE RACE IS ALMOST OVER!" or "JUST FIVE MORE MINUTES!" But wouldn't that be nice? He doesn't deny that the race is hard and sacrificial, and Jesus didn't mince words when he talked about it.

He said we'd lose our lives: "If anyone would come after me, let him deny himself and take up his cross and follow me. For whoever would save his life will lose it, but whoever loses his life for my sake and the gospel's will save it" (Mark 8:34, 35).

He said it'd be hard: "Enter by the narrow gate. For the gate is wide and the way is easy that leads to destruction, and those who enter by it are many. For the gate is narrow and the way is hard that leads to life, and those who find it are few" (Matthew 7:13-14).

Much to my chagrin, no matter how much I've searched the Scriptures looking for it, I can't find the verse where Jesus says, "Come, follow me, and I will make your life easy and nothing bad will ever happen to you." Jesus made no implications that following him would lead to a comfortable and luxurious life; he made it pretty clear that the opposite, in fact, was on its way.

I will be the first to admit that I am a lazy, comfort-loving sinner. I battle daily with my desires of the flesh and my love for the things of this world. I forget the mission Jesus gave his disciples on a regular basis. But I feel it in my bones and in my spirit: **it's time for us to wake up and run**. It's time for us to stop living for ourselves and live the lives Jesus created us to live.

It is *not* going to be easy. I often get caught up in what this world has to offer. I love feeling comfortable. I am easily distracted. And I give up *so* easily, friends. But this life, this life of saying yes to Jesus, is so worth the cost. And he is patient and gentle with us. He loves a willing and obedient heart, even when we mess up sometimes. So if you're afraid to say yes to Jesus' next invitation for you, just tell him! He can handle it. Ask for strength, courage, and boldness. Be honest.

I believe in a gracious and merciful God. I believe in a God who is slow to anger, abounding in steadfast love and faithfulness (Exodus 34:6–7). I believe in a God who is jealous for you (Exodus 20:5). Who loves you (Romans 8:35, 38–39). Who wants to be with you (John 15:4–5). Who wants to do great things in you and through you (Ephesians 2:10). I believe God wants you to see yourself the way he sees you (Ephesians 4:22–24). I believe in a God who is *so good* that he sent his own beloved Son to die a cursed death just so you and I could have the chance to spend eternity in his presence (John 3:16).

And I do believe this God is *worth following*. He's a God worth laying down *my life* for.

I am not perfect, not even close. I reject invitations from Jesus on the daily, but I'm learning to love Jesus more than I love the world. Slowly (very slowly), but surely. And God is so patient with us, so gracious. He doesn't quit on us when we quit on him. He doesn't revoke the status of our salvation when we do say no. He doesn't withhold his love from us when we are disobedient. He gives us second, third, and thirty-seventh chances. He walks with us at our pace, guiding us along hand in hand the whole way because he's just that good and just that loving. I don't know that I'll ever understand, but I'm thankful he doesn't expect perfection of us.

02

yes to restoration

I t all started in a greenhouse. Not an actual greenhouse, mind you, but an imaginary one. Close your eyes and picture it with me (but only after you read this paragraph, of course, unless by chance someone is reading this aloud to you): there it is, over there, surrounded by an ethereal wooded forest, shiny blue glass, absolutely bursting with an overgrown garden inside. It doesn't appear to have been properly tended for a hot minute. Blooming dahlias and tall sunflowers and thick green bushes abound, roses with too many thorns, maybe some ferns and a tall skinny tree over there, to the left. If you're into gardening, unlike me, you might stop here with a frown and think, "Why are all of those things in the same garden at the same time?" But this is my imagination, okay? Stick with me.

If you look a little closer, you'll also find the wild-spreading dandelions, the morning glory that is almost impossible to get rid of, and some random patches of other weeds. I didn't even know weeds could get inside greenhouses, but apparently they can. The most peculiar thing about this greenhouse, though, is not what is inside, but that someone has seemingly been boarding it up over time, bit by bit, covering the glass panes with mismatched wooden planks—some old and weathered, some that still smell fresh like the lumber section at the Home Depot. Some have been painted in bright colors. And the garden inside, though appearing to be brimming with life, is slowly dying, suffocating for lack of sunlight, begging for a little care and attention.

I came upon this greenhouse in my mind's eye in the summertime of 2017. I was 24, and I was preparing for an adventure of a lifetime: I would soon be leaving my job as a graphic designer in Wichita, Kansas, for a ten-month mission trip. First stop, Canada for two months of intensive discipleship training; next stop, somewhere overseas for seven months of serving. Little did I know that this adventure would be much longer than ten months.

Although I was excited, I was nervous. And maybe more than nervous, I was scared. I'm a fairly private person, avoiding the spotlight and the center of attention. I'm an internal processor who struggles to name my own emotions. I'm not a fan of crying in front of people or sharing my innermost thoughts with people. Especially strangers. (So, why did I write a book again?) Yet, I knew this training was no joke, and I should take it seriously. But I was scared of what God wanted to do in me; I was scared of what might be brought to light. I was nervous to be embarrassed in front of my peers, like maybe some deep dark stuff inside me would come to light that I didn't even know about. I was set on preserving my reputation as a good leader and a good Christian girl who had it all together, but I wanted to be open to what God had for me. Unfortunately, it is very hard to have open hands when you're clinging tightly to what you are already holding. And I quite liked what I was holding.

Anyway, there I was, stumbling through this fairytale-like forest in my mind when I saw the greenhouse. I stopped, crossed my arms, and looked at it with a furrowed brow. I knew immediately that this greenhouse was a picture of my heart. I pursed my lips and exhaled slowly.

I cautiously approached the greenhouse and considered what was before me. My fear of letting others in as I tried to uphold my reputation was leading me on an unfortunate trajectory. I was hiding behind a carefully crafted exterior, too afraid of what might happen should they see my heart. Should my garden be too beautiful, would someone hurt it? Steal it? Kill it? Should my garden be an overgrown and unkempt mess (as it was now), would I be put to shame? Rather than put my heart at risk, I had subconsciously decided to conceal it from the world altogether to avoid all of the above. I was the one who had been boarding up this greenhouse. Me.

I carefully circled the house, inspecting the wooden planks and making note of many behaviors and coping mechanisms used to keep others at arm's length. I had hammered those boards up one by one, using humor to deflect pain, escaping reality into fictional television shows and books, keeping a busy schedule, and avoiding negative emotions in general. I knew I needed to change. I didn't want to keep hiding behind my exterior; I wanted Jesus to shine forth from my interior. I wanted to tear down those boards and light them all on fire. I wanted to call up the Gardener and invite him to somehow fix this mess, but I didn't know where to even begin.

* * *

The thing about Jesus, our Gardener in this story, is that he wants to *restore* us, not just *fix* us. And that's a slow, steady process. Slower than most of us have patience for. What's the difference, though, between fixing and restoring? I heard it put this way once: when you fix a car, you simply buy new parts to replace the old parts that didn't work. Or, in my case, I pay somebody to do that. I know nothing about cars, except that they have four wheels and they get me where I want to go.

When you restore a car, however, the intent is to bring it back to the original design, to its former glory, if you will. You put time and effort and money into finding original parts, and you won't settle for less. I don't imagine that someone who is serious about restoring his or her 1964 Ford Mustang would put a piece from 1999 in that car. (Yes, I just web-searched "popular old cars to restore." Judge me.) Likewise, Jesus wants to restore us into who he originally intended us to be. We were created with purpose, for purpose, but we live in this messed up, chaotic world of distraction and sin and brokenness. Rather than simply fixing what has been broken with a mishmash of different parts, Jesus wants to redeem and restore those things to what they were before sin entered our world.

Going back to the gardening analogy, this means that there is much work to be done. Our Gardener is not going to just run a lawn mower over us and start over. In the same way, he won't just start throwing seeds into a messy garden and hope that everything works out. Weeds must be identified and pulled up from the root, good fruit and flowers can be salvaged or transplanted, soil must be cared for. He won't just let dead flowers stay; he won't let thriving weeds stick around either.

But hear this: we have to be willing. Our God so desperately wants to work in us and restore us and tend our gardens, but he won't move until we invite him. He isn't forceful or harsh with us; we serve a humble and kind and gentle Gardener. He wants to work *with us* in this. Perhaps this restoration process is what many of us call "sanctification," the process of becoming more holy, more like Jesus. Just as a tree won't bear fruit overnight, nor does our sanctification happen instantly; it's an ongoing journey that takes our entire lives.

God doesn't put all the work on us, but he's not going to do it all for us either. When we try to become more like Jesus on our own, it becomes all about behavior management. Not doing this, staying away from that, creating boundaries to stay within and rules to live by. That doesn't sound a whole lot like freedom to me. But, on the other hand, if we sit there and pray, "God, help me not to sin anymore," and we go about doing anything and everything we feel like, we will likely not come any closer to holiness. Gardener God is in charge of the weeding and pruning process, but we are his co-laborers, and our hearts and our souls and our very lives are his garden.

* * *

The very beginning started with a garden, after all. "And the Lord God planted a garden in Eden, in the east, and there he put the man whom he had formed" (Genesis 2:8). Humankind and our very own livelihood started in the garden, and God filled it with beautiful plants and "took the man and put him in the garden of Eden to work it and keep it." (2:15). It was always a joint process from the very beginning—us and God. But it didn't used to be so *hard*.

In the townhouse where I currently live, we have a very unattractive shared garden space out back. My roommates and I complain about the eyesore often, though we do absolutely nothing about it. Weeds, patches of sparse grass, rocks and wood chips, dead tree stumps, etc. are strewn about the lawn. Some kids in our complex tried to plant flowers this last spring, but they quickly lost interest when they weren't seeing results. They watered for about a week or two, but nothing came up. What they didn't take into consideration, however, was the condition of the soil.

I won't claim to be a gardener or a soil expert of any kind, but I could tell you after one quick glance from my kitchen window twenty feet away that this soil is not good for breeding or sustaining any kind of life. It's hard, even after a good rain, and it's about fifty percent gravel. In all my research, in all my internet surfing and blog reading, one thing that I've learned for certain is this: *the key to a healthy garden is healthy soil.*

The soil is where the nutrients are. The soil is what cultivates life! In the creation story, we see that God formed nearly every living thing from the ground! "The LORD God formed the man of dust from the ground" (Genesis 2:7). "Out of the ground the LORD God made to spring up every tree that is pleasant to the sight and good for food" (2:9). "Out of the ground the LORD God had formed every beast of the field and every bird of the heavens" (2:19). The ground on which we walk, the soil in which we plant, cannot be ignored.

In the Garden of Eden, God gave man and woman some pretty clear instructions, not to eat from one specific tree, and, well, they didn't obey. Sin, often defined as "missing the mark" or disobedience, entered the story and entered our world. And sin is the culprit behind hardened soil. The rocks and the gravel and the clay that make it so hard for crops to thrive, the thorns and thistles that choke them, and the weeds that rob nutrients are all results of sin. "'Cursed is the ground because of you,'" God told a disobedient Adam (Genesis 3:17). Our failure to obey makes the ground hard to work with; it stunts our growth. It makes it difficult to even plant new seeds. It takes a whole lot of work to maintain healthy soil. Sometimes it even requires a breaking.

* * *

When I invited the Gardener to come renovate my greenhouse, I didn't realize the years of intensive labor I was in for. Remember, sanctification takes a lifetime. I thought I was just asking him to come remove some old ugly boards, and the glass underneath would be shiny and new, and the garden inside would magically figure itself out. In actuality, when the boards started to come down, it was revealed that some of the glass was shattered, some of the flowers inside were suffering, weeds were spreading, and some soil was compromised. It was time to get my hands dirty.

Knocking down those boards required putting down my defenses, getting vulnerable in community, and being honest when I'm struggling. Asking for help has never come easy for me. I am so good at faking that I'm fine, that sometimes even I believe myself. God created us to live in community for a reason. We aren't meant to do this whole thing on our own, but Satan likes to make us feel that way. I was so afraid for so long of what others thought of me that I just kept quiet.

When confession in community became a more regular rhythm in my life, my eyes were opened to how I had let the enemy make me feel very alone in the past. I often thought that surely I was the only one who thought like this, struggled with that, felt this way. Surely I was crazy. But then a couple of girls and I started meeting together fairly regularly to confess and pray together. And we found that we thought a lot of the same things. We struggled in similar areas. We could relate. And we would always walk away from those times of sharing saying, "Well, at least I'm not crazy!"

I let Satan silence me for too long, and not only was I afraid to speak out about the hard things, but I also became afraid to speak out about the beautiful and powerful things. Words of encouragement and affirmation, words that empower and strengthen. The enemy pinpoints and attacks the very tools God has given us to build up his Kingdom, hoping to distract us and scare us out of doing the good works God prepared in advance for us to do (Ephesians 2:10).

I believe that God wants me to use my words for his glory; writing and speaking and encouraging and teaching are tools he has given me, and when I'm not using them, the enemy celebrates. Psalm 32:3 says, "For when I kept silent, my bones wasted away through my groaning all day long." Silence is sometimes easier, but it can slowly gnaw away at us, leaving us to waste away alone.

Whether or not you feel like God has gifted you in writing or speaking or teaching, don't let the enemy silence you. There is something powerful about confessing, worshiping, and praying out loud, especially in a group setting. There are definitely times and places to be alone, to be silent in the greenhouse, just you and God, carefully tending to your soul garden. But there are definitely times and places to be in community with other believers. Do not shy away from it; invite trusted others into your digging, your planting, your weeding, and your blooming. Don't let them *become* the Gardener, but simply an extra pair of working hands, pointing out a weed here, a lovely flourishing flower there. Let them water you with words of encouragement and plant new seeds, as fellow co-laborers in maintaining healthy soil that gives life to our hearts and souls. And when the ground needs to be broken, you won't have to suffer alone.

03

yes to discomfort

"Go from your country and your kindred and your father's house to the land that I will show you,'" was the calling Abram received from God (Genesis 12:1). I felt the LORD invite me into a similar calling when I signed up to go on a ten-month mission program called TREK, except I tried really hard to read between the lines, and I was pretty sure I saw the word "Peru" written in there somewhere.

I went to Peru the first time when I was eighteen, and then again at age twenty-one, both on six-week mission trips. Peru was a sacred place of transformation for me; it's the place where I learned to be independent, to not be so afraid, to not let my age or abilities limit the LORD and his work; it's the place where I truly learned to pray, where I heard the Holy Spirit speak for the first time, and where I first felt at home away from home.

I was the girl in college who was obsessed with Peru. Not so much because of the actual place, I have realized now, but because of what had happened in that place. I wore my Peru hoodie and carried my Peru purse proudly, and I was probably [read: definitely] the person who told way too many stories that started with, "One time, in Peru..." I started listening to Spanish worship songs in my car, and I still have a little pin on my backpack of the Peruvian flag.

When I signed up for TREK, I didn't know where they would place me to serve, but I was confident that it would be Peru. How could it *not* be Peru? There was no way. I was the Peru girl, remember? You should have seen all the friendship bracelets on my wrist! I knew the options were Peru, Thailand, Myanmar, and Canada. Myanmar was looking to be an all-boys team, and I was pretty sure Canada was off the table for me. That narrowed it down to Peru and Thailand. *I did not want to go to Thailand.* I knew way too many people who went to Thailand, and they were all weirdly obsessed with it. I wanted to be weirdly obsessed with Peru. I told everyone I trusted God, though. I really thought I did. I trusted that God would let me go to Peru.

* * *

I had two friends applying for the program as well: Catherine and Karen. We had all been to Peru before, and we all wanted to go back. We were all die-hard Peru girls. I remember telling Catherine that I was so afraid that I would be asked to lead the Thailand team. What would I do then, say no? The program staff selected three or four team leaders each year before training started. I had a feeling, having led a team before and knowing some of the program staff personally, that my chances of being asked to lead a team were high. But they would ask me to lead the team to Peru, right?

A few days after I visited that imaginary boarded-up greenhouse (see the last chapter if you forgot what I'm referring to already), I received The Email. The Email that began this long journey in understanding what it means to be obedient.

I was at work when it slid into my inbox. I opened it, seeing that it was from the program director, addressed to both Karen and me. The more I read, the further my heart sank into my stomach. I felt like

I was going to throw up. The Email was an invitation to talk with him about being team leaders. But there was a catch: they needed one leader to go to Peru, and one leader to go to Thailand. My worst nightmare was becoming a reality.

I was a wreck for a week, thinking about what would happen if I had to go to Thailand. The whole reason I signed up for TREK was to go to Peru. I couldn't concentrate on anything else leading up to the meeting with the program director, Fred.

I came to the meeting prepared with a whole list of reasons why I should either (a) not be a team leader at all, or (b) co-lead the Peru team with Karen. Five minutes into the conversation, it was obvious that I couldn't say no to being a team leader; the job description was a perfect fit for me. I quickly looked at my list of reasons why we should be co-leaders, but Fred cut me off. He said he was taking Thailand off the table for me. I should lead the Peru team. It just made sense, and we agreed that it seemed that God was leading me in this direction.

A few minutes later I hung up and jumped out of the blue chair in the corner of my bedroom. I was overjoyed! I couldn't believe it. I was going to Peru. For seven months. Hallelujah! I threw my hands in the air, praising God, and then before I knew it, I was face down in my dirty brown carpet, crying. And these were not happy tears.

That's when the anxiety sunk in. I felt like I was going to throw up again. I was restless, nauseous, couldn't think straight. My family was confused. Isn't this what I wanted? Yes, yes this is exactly what I wanted. So why didn't I feel excited?

For hours I felt sick to my stomach. My mind and my heart were racing. Something was wrong, very wrong.

I went to bed and woke up at 2:00 am in a literal sweat. My insides felt twisted up, like a wet washcloth ready to wring out. I was too tired for this. I told God we'd talk about it in the morning; could I please get some sleep? He conceded. I went back to sleep.

The next morning I woke up feeling good, but then I remembered. I sat down in my corner chair to pray and read my Bible. I can't quite explain to you the complete turmoil I felt in my soul and spirit. *Had I made the wrong decision?* As I tried to concentrate on the Scriptures, I glanced up at a picture I had hung up on my bookshelf.

A few years before I had drawn a cartoon picture of myself on a piece of paper, and several girls I knew and loved from women's ministry in college wrote encouraging notes all around the edges. Words about how I was full of joy and love. As I skimmed this piece of paper for the hundredth time, the comment that stuck out the most read, "You encourage me! Never be afraid to be who God has called you to be and go where he has called you." Tears welled up in my eyes.

* * *

In the story of the Exodus, there's a really powerful moment when the LORD tells Moses to split the Red Sea so that the Israelites can walk across on dry ground, escaping the Egyptians who are following closely behind (Exodus 14). This is a pretty popular story, and if you grew up around the church, I'm sure you've heard it more times than you can count. If you haven't, I highly recommend you go read it. The part of the story I never really noticed before, though, is actually right before the Israelites arrive at the Red Sea.

Exodus 13:17-18 reads, "When Pharaoh let the people go, God did not lead them by the way of the land of the Philistines, although that was near. For God said, 'Lest the people change their minds when they see war and return to Egypt.' But God led the people around by the way of the wilderness toward the Red Sea." God took the Israelites not by the obvious, closest route to Canaan, but by the roundabout, circuitous way through the wilderness that led them to the Red Sea. If you look at a map, you'll notice almost immediately that to get from Egypt to Canaan, it is not necessary, like *at all*, to cross the Red Sea. In fact it's a whole lot shorter not to.

Imagine yourself in the sandals of an Israelite. You trusted Moses, trusted God, to take you to Canaan. Now here you are on this seemingly wild-goose chase. The Egyptians are approaching, and you're at the shore, staring into a giant body of water. Why are you even here? Why didn't Moses just leave you to die in Egypt? Anxiety fills your chest; the panic bells are going off in your brain. You need to make a decision, and fast. Should you turn around? Should you just start swimming?

* * *

I stared at that piece of paper taped to my bookshelf and gulped. I waited a beat, took a deep breath, and nervously asked God aloud, "I can't be this person you've called me to be *and* go to Peru right now, can I?"

Cue the tears. And cue the peace flooding my heart.

"I think I have to go to Thailand," I whispered to myself. I cried some more.

At the time, it was as if I was on the shore like the Israelites trying to make this decision. Going to Peru felt a lot like trying to swim the Red Sea: exhausting, but isn't that where God had led me? I tried to imagine ten whole months of anxiety and nausea. That didn't sound like fun at all. That didn't sound like a good use of my time. Just one day earlier Peru had seemed like the obvious choice, but in this moment it was as if the sea parted and there in front of me was the Red Sea Road, all the way to Thailand.

I had always trusted God, but I realized that much of that was because he had never asked me to do anything so hard before. He had really never asked me to do something I didn't want to do. He had never asked me to completely lay down my dreams. My trust in God was solely based on the fact that he had always given me everything I ever wanted. Could I trust him in this? Could I trust that when he says he has something better in store for me, he's telling the truth? That he's still faithful, even when I don't get what I want?

God took the Israelites through the wilderness because he was preparing them for what they would face in the years to come. He knew they weren't ready yet for battle. He knew they would want to turn around and give up. In hindsight, my decision wasn't really about Peru or Thailand. God didn't end up calling me to serve long-term in Thailand (not yet, anyway…I've learned to never say never with God), nor did I come back weirdly obsessed with Thailand like everyone else I know (thank goodness). This was about learning to trust God more than it was about going to Thailand. It was about learning to obey, learning to follow. This wouldn't be the last time God invited me to do something I really didn't want to do. He was training me for what was ahead in the years to come.

* * *

I've said it before, and I'll say it again: following Jesus gets a lot harder when Jesus starts going to uncomfortable places. The farther he gets from our comfort zones, the more we hesitate to step out. Really, Jesus? There? You want me to go *there*? It doesn't always make sense. Sometimes it even seems counterintuitive. He'll take you the long way, the roundabout way, the scary way, the nearly impossible way. He might take you to Peru, just to get you to Thailand! He'll have you cross the Red Sea to get to Canaan! It seems straight up crazy at times. But it's in those moments, I think, that we're forced to come face to face with a question that Jesus asked two of his disciples at the very beginning of their friendship: "What are you seeking?" (John 1:38).

This question has wrecked me time and time again. In this passage, we have John the Baptist standing with two of his disciples. Jesus walks by, and John yells out, "Behold, the Lamb of God!" (John 1:29). I imagine the disciples looking around for an actual sheep here maybe, shrugging at each other in confusion. I know I would. But the text says they actually started following Jesus after hearing John say this. Like, literally following him. Walking behind him. Maybe trying to figure out who this guy is.

And Jesus, sweet Jesus, doesn't ignore them or pretend he doesn't see them or blow them off. "Jesus turned and saw them following and said to them, 'What are you seeking?'" (John 1:38). He turns and sees them. Sees their interest. Sees their hunger and desire and curiosity. Sees their willingness, perhaps. And so he speaks. "What are you seeking?" Or, maybe in other words, "Why are you following me?"

I think sometimes Jesus does this with me, and you, too. He turns, looks me kindly in the eye, and asks, "Hey, Becky, girl, why are you following me? What is it you're seeking? Your own glory? Your own comfort? Or my glory?"

I picture Jesus walking slow and steady down a path, a slightly amused look on his face. I'm behind him quite a ways, and I'm trying to pick up all this stuff off the ground as I go, and it's slowing me down. I'm a little nervous that I might trip, so I bend down to check my shoelaces a few too many times. It's a little hot out, so I readjust my hat and reapply my sunscreen.

And Jesus is just chuckling and whistling and humming as he walks, waiting for me to catch up and take his hand. But at some point he gently turns and catches my attention. "Baby girl, what are you seeking? Why are you following me even though you clearly don't want to?"

Oh, man. He knows!? I freeze, caught in the middle of crouching low to pick up something I've dropped. I slowly stand, miscellaneous objects I've picked up along the way falling out of my hands and pockets. He motions for me to come next to him and puts his warm hand on my shoulder. "What is it you're seeking? Why are you following me?"

Why *are* you following? When life is fine and dandy, you may not think much about the why. But when you're in the wilderness, you've got to preach it to yourself. Why is this worth it? Is it? Is the pain and the hardship really worth what lies on the other side? What are you seeking?

04

yes to losing myself

Insecurity. Let's talk about it. We all struggle with it, or have struggled with it at some point in our lives. Even those people you follow on Instagram who seem to have perfect skin and perfect teeth and the perfect family and the perfect little puppy—they're insecure, too. Why? This is a question I have found myself asking over the last few years. What do we have to be insecure about? What is it rooted in? And what does "security" even look like?

When the world talks about insecurity, it's typically related to our looks or our self-esteem or how we carry ourselves. I'm sure we can all relate to these kinds of insecurities. I know I can. The world says the antidote to those feelings is simply to make ourselves better. To improve ourselves. To make a name for ourselves. To find ourselves. But those are just temporary fixes for a deeper problem. Even beautiful, successful, happy people can be, and usually are, insecure.

In the mic-drop-worthy words of my friend Carla, "Insecurity is a sign that you don't believe who God says you are is true." Woof. Let that sink in. I believe, at its root, insecurity is primarily tied to two things: identity crisis and fear of man. When you don't know who you are—which is who God says you are—you will never be confident in your own skin because you will always chase after who others say you need to be, and you will always be afraid of disappointing them.

Unfortunately for many of us, this turns into an exhausting guessing game. We aren't mind readers; we don't really know what others expect of us, and so we jump from one persona to the next, trying to make others happy. We can't simply ask, for fear of *appearing* insecure or weak or stupid. And then we just get tired. Sick of ourselves. Barely able to recognize the person in the mirror because somehow we know this isn't who we were made to be, even though we don't know who that really is.

I'm tired just thinking about it.

But thanks be to God, we weren't meant to live this way.

So how *do* we "find ourselves?" In the movies, the girl always chops off all her hair and moves to New York City and wears cute overalls and discovers her love for sculpting and opens her own art studio instead of becoming a lawyer like her father wanted. Is that all it takes? A new haircut and New York City?

* * *

It was at TREK training that I realized I didn't know who I was. I didn't know my identity. I was tired of trying to be everyone else. For so long I had been so content with living small. I flew under the radar, revealing very little of myself to others. I lived a quiet life, afraid of disrupting peace. Afraid of not meeting the expectations of others. If people didn't notice me, though, they couldn't have expectations for me not to meet.

Comfort, a form of false peace, was my idol. I pushed negative emotions away, I buried any anger, and quite honestly, I *was* actually happy. I exuded joy and cheerfulness and confidence, and I genuinely did not feel like I was faking it.

However, the consequence of living within the confines of your comfort zone is a small and shallow life, where fear dictates every move and slowly takes over the throne. It is very difficult to follow Jesus from your comfort zone. It is very difficult to be obedient to Jesus when the god you serve actually goes by the name "happiness." It is very difficult to find yourself when you aren't willing to search very far.

I see now that I was afraid for God to notice me out of fear that I would fall short of his expectations for my life. I hung my head low in his presence. My prayers were nervous and hesitant. I often wrote my prayers, avoiding direct conversation with him. I was afraid of disappointing God, not measuring up to his standards, and being flat-out rejected. I am still recovering from the habit I call self-disqualification; I prematurely take myself out of the game so nobody else can do it for me. This habit was formed by lies I believed about myself and about God. It was formed because of my lack of security in who God says I am.

In one of our training sessions, the teacher drew a line down the middle of the whiteboard at the front of the room; on the left, we compiled a list of what the world says about identity. Things like appearance, where we come from, career, success, money, connections, and material possessions filled this side of the board. The right side was a list of things God says about our identity, straight from the Scripture: loved, holy and blameless, adopted into sonship, free, the list goes on.

The bottom line is this: the things the world says define us are all based on things we do. And they can change tomorrow. One car accident, one mishap that leaves us jobless, one natural disaster could change everything. The rich and famous can easily become nobodies at the drop of a hat. Likewise, the wallflowers and shadow-lurkers can easily become somebodies with one viral video on the internet.

On the other hand, what God says our identity is based on, simply put, has nothing to do with us. My identity has absolutely nothing to do with me, and everything to do with Christ. Therefore, my identity can never be changed, lost, or stolen. For me, this revelation was, in a word, transformative. Nothing I ever do can change who I am. Likewise, nothing the enemy or the world does can take that away either. I simply am who God says I am. And that's that.

That's not to say that people don't change. I am a firm believer that people do. But my personality or my character or my habits don't define my identity in the way that God does. Those things define my reputation.

I'd like to say it took only this one session for me to get it, but it didn't. Coming to the realization that I was having an identity crisis wasn't a long process. Feeling secure in that identity is taking a little longer.

*　*　*

I left for Thailand, determined to "find myself." To feel rooted and secure in my identity in Christ, whatever that meant. The first month was hard. I felt lonely and unsure. Fearful. Uncomfortable. Tired. I was afraid that God would call me to move to Thailand forever. Afraid of the plans he had for me. Afraid of his calling.

One night I remember being in my very pink room on my knees, face to the floor. I didn't want to be in Thailand anymore. It had been only three weeks. I had six months left. I asked God for the hundredth time why he sent me to this place instead of Peru. And that day, I felt like he actually gave me an answer.

This was to be a time of stripping. He wanted to show me who I really was, who he had made me to be. He was stripping me of comfort.

Of familiar language. Of being able to go wherever I wanted, and eat whenever and whatever. He was stripping me of familiar friends and family. He was stripping me of my false sense of security. I was sweating all the time, my face was constantly breaking out, and I brought all the wrong clothes. I felt awkward and underqualified.

But God—oh, what a lovely phrase—wanted to make me into something beautiful. A rich color palette of light pink and olive green and powder blue and mustard yellow, with a little bit of glittery gold. A poem, a painting, a song, a sculpture. He was chiseling and chipping away at my figure, reforming a few curves here, refining a few joints there, where I had let too many other artists formerly hold the chisel and carve away as they pleased.

Away from the noise, away from the familiar, who was Becky? Something about being "here, right now" was going to make me more into the Becky Spahr he had created me to be.

*　*　*

Here's the thing: you won't believe you are who God says you are if you don't believe God is who he says he is. Did you follow that?

In other words: if you don't know who God is, you won't know who you are.

In *other* other words: if you don't trust God, you will always struggle with insecurity.

I spent a couple of months in Thailand trying to figure out who I was. I read the verses about being chosen, being loved, being free, etc. Nothing was really hitting home for me, though. Then, the day after Christmas, I saw an email in my inbox with the subject line that read, "Stop trying to find yourself."

With great curiosity I opened this particular email and watched the attached video. I blinked, feeling conviction all the way to my toes as the narrator said, "This journey we call life is not about finding ourselves so much as it is about *losing ourselves and finding Him*" (emphasis mine).[1]

I was going about this all wrong. I had been so focused on myself, when the whole time, I should have been focused on discovering who God is! It finally clicked. Our goal in life is to be more like Jesus. How can we be like Jesus if we don't know who Jesus is? And likewise, how could I believe who God says I am if I don't have an understanding of God's character? If I trust that God is who he says he is—good, faithful, loving, true, just—then I can't *not* believe him when he says I am worthy, loved, his daughter, forgiven. I needed to stop searching for who I am and start seeking the Great I AM.

* * *

There's another story in Exodus, before the whole Red Sea incident, that I come back to in every major event of my life: the story of Moses and the burning bush. If you've ever heard me share a devotion, preach a sermon, or share my testimony, there's a seventy-five percent chance you've heard me talk about this story. Moses is my homeboy, and this story rocks my world.

Let me take you to Exodus chapter three this time. Moses is minding his own business, keeping his father-in-law's flock when he notices a bush on fire, but it's not actually burning up. Curious, he approaches the bush. I think what the Bible says Moses said is kind of hilarious, "'I will turn aside to see this great sight, why the bush is not burned'" (3:3). Do you think he actually said that out loud to himself and the sheep?

Anyway, he approaches the bush and is instructed to take off his sandals (oh, how I wish I could dive deeper into all of this for you, but now is not the time), and the living and breathing God introduces himself to Moses in an audible voice. Chills. Literal chills. And God straight-up tells Moses that he is supposed to go to Pharaoh and bring the Israelites out of slavery and out of Egypt. And just as an aside, get this: Moses is 80 years old. If you're 18 or 25 or 45 and feeling bad because you don't know your calling, take heart. Moses didn't know until he was literally elderly.

Now, we're approaching my point here; Moses is taken aback. He asks God, "'Who am I that I should go to Pharaoh and bring the children of Israel out of Egypt?'" (3:11). Moses is thinking God must have the wrong guy. Long story short, Moses grew up in Pharaoh's palace, but then he murdered a guy and ran away, and now he's just a shepherd. What would make God think that Moses of all people could do this? To top off all that, Moses had some kind of speech impediment (4:10).

But rather than encourage Moses by reminding him of all the ways he is talented and gifted and why he's the perfect man for this job, God's response is simply, "'But I will be with you'" (3:12). In other words, "It's not about you, Moses!" God completely disregards Moses' question, "Who am I?" and reminds Moses who he's talking to. It's not about us and who we are; it's always about him and who he is.

**

To get to know Jesus more, I started reading the Bible through a different lens. I know it may come as a shock, but the Bible isn't actually about us. It's about God! Who knew? I started reading less to "apply it to my own life" and more to understand the character of God. What does God do? What does God say? What is God like?

It's funny how as humans we can make anything and everything about us. My eyes were suddenly open to how even my relationship with the LORD was about me. Worship, I had somehow twisted to be about what I could get out of it. How would the LORD speak to *me* in this time? Prayer was about how *I* felt. Teaching from the Word was about how smart I sounded.

I am getting convicted all over again just writing this.

When you're in relationship with another human being, if the relationship is all about you, the other person begins to grow weary. God cares for us; let's care for him, too.

When you concentrate purely on your half of your relationship with God, it starts to become less than a relationship. It becomes about managing behaviors, becoming a "better person," feeling "less guilty," doing more for God, maintaining an image of spirituality, talking the talk and trying to walk the walk out of our own strength.

But when you focus on God, the other person in the relationship, it changes things. It becomes about his glory. His good. His honor. His name. His heart for people. It becomes about love. You start to let him make you more like himself. You start to surrender.

We are created in his image, in his likeness. As believers, we carry his name. We are his children, his sons and daughters. Co-heirs with Christ, adopted into sonship. Friend, have security in knowing that you are his. You belong to him. Nothing can snatch you from his hand. Not the devil, not the darkness. Trust him when he says he loves you. When he says he will never leave you nor forsake you. His Word is good and true.

05

yes to the mission

I've heard the spiel dozens of times over the years. In fact, I've even given the spiel. If you've ever been on a short-term mission trip, I'm sure you've heard it too: *The mission trip doesn't end with the trip... We can still "live on mission" in our home context... Our backyards are the mission field!* It became like that song that's overplayed on the radio; one day you're at the mall and singing along while you look for the perfect nail polish color and suddenly your eyes widen as you wonder, "How do I know all the words to this song?" And for the first time you actually listen to the lyrics and understand what the song means. All that to say, I had the spiel memorized backwards and forwards, but it took a minute, or more like ten years, to actually click.

Being a "missionary" in the United States, or even Canada for that matter, never really appealed to me. To be frank, it was too hard. In comparison to the people I had met on the short trips I had been on, North Americans seemed less receptive to a casual chat about Jesus on the street or an invitation to church. In my mind, it would be much easier to be a missionary somewhere overseas.

***

I was forced into my first gospel conversation with a stranger. It was 2015, and my roommate Carly and I thought we were going to a prayer walk, and I suppose it was one, but not like we imagined. One evening we were invited to join a few people to walk around a university campus and pray, and we had no other plans, so we thought, why not?

We met up with the group at our church first (which turned out to be just two other people), and the guy in charge said something about praying with strangers, with students. Carly and I looked at each other in alarm. We drove the twenty minutes to the campus in almost complete silence, hearts beating out of our chests. We had to talk to strangers!? We had to pray with students? We thought we were just praying *for* students. We would not have come tonight if we had known. We *could* just drive home…

As tempting as it was, we did not drive home. We reconvened at the school and started walking as a group, the leader showing us how easy it really was. He asked someone for directions to the student center (we really didn't know where it was), and then told him we were walking around praying for people; could we pray for him? And it was that simple.

We split off into pairs then, and set out to find more people to pray for. I spent almost the entire evening talking to a student who also happened to be a Christian. She was so encouraged by our boldness that she asked if she could join us next time we came to pray on campus.

Carly and I left the campus that evening with a new fire in our bellies. Neither of us had ever done anything like that before, even though we had both been on a plethora of mission trips. It wasn't hard; it wasn't even that intrusive. People were allowed to say no and walk away, and it wasn't a big deal. But others had questions that led to good conversation. I think that was the night that both of us understood for the first time that we really could do this. We could actually "live on mission" in our own city. We could share the gospel. We could point people to Jesus.

Talking to complete strangers at the park or university or shopping mall is *not* the only way to live on mission; please do not hear me say that! But even if you aren't planning on going door to door to evangelize to all of your neighbors, you still have to know the gospel and be able to articulate it. What happens if the next time you're picking up your take-out, someone walks right up to you and asks where you find your hope? Your joy? Your peace? Will you have an answer? Our boy Peter says we need to always be prepared "to make a defense to anyone who asks you for a reason for the hope that is in you; yet do it with gentleness and respect" (1 Peter 3:15). And even if you've been a Christian for twenty years, that requires a little thought and a little practice.

You don't have to preach a sermon; you don't have to draw a fancy little diagram or picture or say it perfectly. But don't be caught with your pants down! Don't fumble for your phone to call your pastor and ask him what to say in that moment. For those of you who are internal processors like me, we have to put in a little work ahead of time for that moment, or we will be found staring wide-eyed, mouth agape like a deer in headlights.

The gospel is the good news of Jesus Christ. What makes it so good? That's the message you need to internalize before you're able to share. If the gospel isn't actually personal for you, it makes talking about it seem very disingenuous. What has Jesus personally done for you? Why are you a Christian? Why are you following the Lord? This takes us back to chapter three: what are you seeking?

When you're able to answer those questions, the gospel is a lot easier to talk about. Jesus has personally saved me from an empty life and a life of fear, and he has given me purpose, identity, and security. That's a pretty relatable topic of conversation, wouldn't you agree? What has he saved you from? What do you love about him?

* * *

Even though I loved going on mission trips throughout high school and college, I never felt like I experienced a moment when God bestowed upon me the "missionary call." I have friends who knew by age eight they were going to be overseas missionaries. I have friends who grew up as missionary kids and swore they would never go overseas again, but ultimately received "the call." I have friends who went on their first mission trip and knew in their hearts and in their bones this is where they were meant to be.

Those are beautiful and true stories, but I am not like those friends. And when I signed up for that ten-month mission program, I was hoping that maybe this would be my moment. The heavens would open, and maybe a dove would even descend, and I would hear the long-awaited words in a booming voice: "Becky Spahr, you are destined to be an overseas missionary (in Peru, of course)!"

Unfortunately, or perhaps *fortunately*, there was a definite flaw in my thinking, and in my perspective on "missionaries" in general. I think many of us define "missionary" as someone who shares the gospel and reaches out to those who don't know Jesus; this is often in a foreign country, and that's probably what comes to mind for many of us. But, why? Why is this particular job title often associated with *location*? We would call someone who delivers letters in Kansas and someone who delivers letters in Moscow the same title: mailman (or woman). Right?

I think we just complicate it too much. Have we just given a fancy title to Christians who actually do what Jesus told all of us to do? Jesus was pretty straightforward in Matthew 28:18-20 when he said, "'All authority in heaven and on earth has been given to me. Go therefore and make disciples of all nations, baptizing them in the name of the Father and of the Son and of the Holy Spirit, teaching them to observe all that I have commanded you. And behold, I am with you always, to the end of the age.'" I don't think Jesus was just talking to the eleven here. That's a pretty big task for eleven dudes (although, they *were* pretty effective)! If we call ourselves followers of Jesus, just as these guys did, we are called to the same things.

In these two verses, Jesus gave us four things to do: go, make disciples, baptize those disciples, and teach them to obey God. A lot of people argue about that first word, "go." Some people believe it is a direct commandment to go to the nations, while some argue that it actually means something more along the lines of "as you are going." Either way, you and I are on the go all the time, whether it's to the grocery store or Thailand or Dallas. *Go where you can*; the location shouldn't hinder the three instructions that follow that word.

Next, Jesus says to make disciples. Not just converts, but disciples. People who *follow* Jesus. What does it even mean to disciple someone? It sounds fancy and like maybe I need a special degree to do it, but I think it's easier than we make it out to be. I think discipling someone just means helping them look more like Jesus. Pouring into them, investing in them, being a good role model for them, encouraging and challenging them, rebuking them when needed. It isn't just meeting with someone for an hour each week, but it's living life with others and inviting them in. In order to disciple, though, one must *be* a disciple of Jesus.

Third: baptize these disciples. Baptism is an outward profession that one has died with Christ and has entered new life with him! Again, we're making disciples, not converts! To stick with someone long enough to see them go all in and be baptized is a little more of a commitment than a five-minute conversation on a Sunday morning!

And last, teach those disciples to observe all that Jesus commanded us. I find it very interesting that this is the final of these instructions from Jesus...Today it can seem like obedience is what we emphasize first and foremost in Western Christianity. We want people to obey now; sometimes at the expense of not meeting Jesus until later. We're uncomfortable with messes in church, and sometimes our message comes across as, "Clean up your act first; then you'll be one of us."

But Jesus first invites us to go to where the people are. Invest in them, share what Jesus did for them. Invite them into the family. Walk with them as they walk with Jesus. And *then* teach them to obey.

To put it plain and simple: if you claim to be a believer, you are called to share the gospel, no matter where you live, and therefore, you *are called* to be a missionary.

The call to disciple, to be a missionary, to follow Jesus is not separate from the rest of our lives. You can be called to be a teacher, a plumber, a fisherman, an astronaut, a chef, a stay-at-home mom, a ministry leader, or anything else, but that does not make you exempt from the call to disciple others.

I pray that you do not hear judgment in my tone as I write this, but encouragement. Because what this means for us is that *we are free to be who God called us to be, and still fulfill his mission.* It means you don't have to be anybody but you. You don't have to move to Africa or

Thailand or Australia to fulfill the mission of God. You don't have to quit your job. You don't have to become a pastor. You don't have to write a book or be an Instagram influencer or a blogger. You don't have to go door to door in your neighborhood. You can use the gifts that the good Lord gave you, and disciple the people he has put in your life today.

***

Our missionary hosts in Thailand were probably some of the most influential women in my life when it comes to understanding how to disciple "as you are going." I watched and lived and worked with these women for seven months, and what I saw was pretty average women who lived pretty normal lives with great intentionality. Even a task as simple as picking up coffee was used as an opportunity to build relationships. Parties and celebrations and game nights were frequent, with both believers and not-yet-believers. Meals were shared; life was shared. We went on runs at the park in the 108 degree weather with our English class students, we tried new coffee shops with friends from the local university, and we frequented the same vendors at the market to chat in limited Thai.

What stood out the most, though, about these women, and about the Thai believers, was their genuine love for their community and the people around them. People were not a project to them. People were people. Friends were friends, whether they believed in the same God or not. They were upfront about who they were and what they were about from the very beginning, and they lived transparent lives. They built relationships out of love and respect, no secret or hidden agendas.

I went to Thailand praying that God would give me a clear answer about whether or not I was supposed to be a long-term missionary. God responded, but not in the way I anticipated. I was called to long-term missions, alright, but God didn't give me a place. He didn't confirm Peru or Thailand or Mexico, or even the USA or Canada. The LORD made it clear to me that no matter where I was headed next, I was to live like this. My calling was not dependent on a place. What I was learning about missions in Thailand could be replicated anywhere. It simply requires love and intentionality.

Go to where people are. Don't wait for them to come to you. And love well. Be a good friend, an honest friend, not a fake friend. If you aren't a Christian and you are my friend, hear me when I say this: I am not your friend because I want to "convert you." I love you, and I'm your friend because I think you are cool and fun, and somehow my brain or my heart or something said, "Them. Choose them," when I met you. But, as your friend, I do think about your eternity and your salvation, and I long for it. Not because I think you're a bad person or something, but because I've tasted and seen the goodness of God, and I just can't keep this to myself.

* * *

Halfway through our time in Thailand, the TREK director came to facilitate a midterm retreat for our team. We went to an island and relaxed on the beach and drank smoothies. Oh, yeah, and we also talked about team conflict and prayed and worshiped together and that kind of thing...But the smoothies were definitely the highlight.

On the last night of our time together, we walked about ten or fifteen minutes down the road from our resort to this beautiful lookout point the girls and I had stumbled upon earlier in the week. The sun was setting, and the blue-green ocean looked so massive that it made me feel microscopic. Some of the boys competed to see who could throw rocks the furthest, and one of the guys took out his guitar. We stood around, staring at the expanse of water, singing together quietly, and then our director felt inspired. He prayed, shared a few words that were on his heart and invited us to make a rock altar, like they often do in the Old Testament, as a commitment to dedicating our lives to the mission of Jesus.

We took a few minutes to silently pray and find our rocks before crafting a small tower. I stared at my rock in my hand as I thought about this commitment. My whole life, for Jesus. For others to know Jesus. Yeah. I was all in. We stood in a straight line facing the ocean and sang about how we were giving up our lives for Jesus and for the world to know him. How it was all for the sake of the world. And we meant it. But it's been harder than I thought, that's for sure.

That song and those lyrics weren't to be taken lightly. It was a vow to walk the Jesus-life. To leave my life as it was and not turn back. I can't help but think of Peter and Andrew when Jesus first called them: "Immediately they left their nets and followed him" (Mark 1:18), and they never turned back. They left their jobs, their entire livelihood. Everything they had ever known. All for Jesus and for his mission.

06
yes to the lonely places

I put down my chocolate muffin and started to cry. Fred sat across from me at the coffee shop, eyes widened. He had just offered me an internship. I felt relief. That's why I was crying. I tried to explain, through my tears and full mouth, that I had been considering another offer. Another internship, one that I really didn't want to do, but I was afraid God would ask me to do. I had sort of, kind of, maybe made a deal with God, that I wasn't going to do the internship unless the supervisor contacted me before February 1. Today was February 2. I hadn't heard from her, and here was Fred, offering me something else.

    I would have to move to Canada, of course, but it would just be for a year. I would work with the short-term mission team, helping plan and train young adults going on mission trips. I could even do some graphic design if I wanted. Writing, social media, teaching, you name it; if I had the skill, I could do it. He gave me six weeks to pray about it with my family. Let's be real though, I didn't need that much time.

    A few weeks later, I emailed Fred with my yes. I was still in Thailand, so upon my return in June, I would go back to Kansas for about six weeks before moving up to British Columbia. There was much work to be done in the meantime. The organization would need to start filling out the proper paperwork pronto in order for me to receive a work permit, and I would need to start fundraising for my salary.

This move involved so many details and so many unknowns, even though I was just going from the US to Canada. I needed the work permit, I needed a car and insurance, I needed a place to live...the list went on forever. Thankfully, the LORD is faithful to provide, and I was able to live with a family and drive their car, both for free! I didn't need furniture or really anything other than my personal belongings. What an answer to prayer.

* * *

Moving to a new city is really hard. Moving to a different country is even harder. I'm the type of person who romanticizes things both before and after they happen, and it pains me to admit that I thought this move was going to be really easy and wonderful. I should know better by now that I'm overly optimistic about this kind of thing. But, I already had some friends up in BC, I knew of a great church, and my job was going to rock. I had visions of me sitting on a cozy couch drinking tea with a bunch of girls, Bibles open, heads thrown back in laughter as we all shared our deepest, darkest secrets. I don't even really like tea. But Canadian Becky, she would like tea.

I moved on August 15, two weeks before we would jump into our two-month intensive training program. We had fifteen young adults coming from four different countries. They would all stay at a retreat center together, and we would spend roughly twelve hours a day, five or six days a week, for two months with them, preparing to send them overseas for seven months. It was intense work, but it was fun work. I was all over the map emotionally during those two months: exhausted, excited, passionate, wiped, anxious, living my best life, fully engaged, ready to be done. We poured our hearts and souls into those guys, and I really did love it, even on the days when I just couldn't wait to go back to bed. I got to do so many different things: teach, cook dinner, plan events, create handouts and booklets, take photos, mentor students, and play games.

But when November came and these fifteen new friends all left to go overseas, I realized how little I had left. My last two months had been completely poured into people who were leaving. Life quickly became very lonely.

* * *

A few days after I moved to BC, I was given an entire day to go be by myself and pray. I went to the ocean, even though the air was thick and the sun was hidden from the nearby wildfires. I just couldn't believe how close it was, a short thirty-minute drive from my new house. This Kansas girl had been landlocked her whole life; it had always been twelve hours to the nearest beach!

I spent the day walking, staring at the ocean and the mountains, and reading my Bible at various coffee shops by the beach. I can't remember why, but I wrote in my journal that I felt like this was the "year of the mountain." Maybe it was the Holy Spirit, or maybe it's just because I was still in awe that I got to watch the sunrise behind the mountains every morning. Either way, it turned out to be significant. I wrote in my journal that day that my heart's desire was to meet with YHWH on the mountain, like Moses, face to face.

Wait, hold up, did somebody say Moses? That's right, folks, we're heading back to Exodus to learn some more about the life of our favorite prophet. (At least, *my* favorite prophet.)

This time we're going to pick up in Exodus 19. If you remember from a few chapters ago, the Israelites crossed the Red Sea in chapter 14. They've already gone through the wilderness of Shur, Marah, Elim, the wilderness of Sin (pretty sure we've all been *there*), Rephidim, and now, in chapter 19, they arrive at Sinai. Like, Mount Sinai. Also casually known as "the mountain of God." The place where God promised Moses, "'When you have brought the people out of Egypt, you shall serve God on this mountain'" (Exodus 3:12). *That Sinai.*

They made it. And Moses set out on his hike up the mountain to meet with God for the first of many conversations on that mountain top.

Have you ever heard the phrase "mountaintop experience" or "mountain high?" This usually refers to having a really intense experience with God, and you're all in, passionate and excited, riding the high of that moment, only for it to fizzle out after a week or two. This was a common occurrence for many of us who grew up going to church camp. (Don't think I'm knocking church camp here. I loved camp. Still do.) We'd sing the songs and jump around and rededicate our lives to Jesus, only to fall back into old habits later that summer. And we'd give up because it was too hard. We didn't "feel" like putting in the work anymore.

I think Moses' mountaintop experiences were a little different. I am sure that those moments were intense. I'm sure Moses rode a little bit of a high afterwards, and I'm sure there were some pretty low lows in between. But something I never considered, especially when I labeled my internship year as "the year of the mountain," is that mountains can be lonely places.

When the Israelites came to Sinai, they camped in the wilderness (also translated as "desert") at the foot of the mountain. Moses ascended alone. No one else was allowed to even touch the edge of the mountain, or they would die (with the exception of Moses' brother Aaron on occasion).

The hike to the top probably took Moses a couple of hours. That's a lot of quality alone time. Sometimes he'd stay up there for days on end. One time it was even forty days (Exodus 24:18). And sometimes he would get to the top, and God would tell him to go back down, tell the people something, and then come back up. Can you imagine your 80-year-old grandpa climbing a mountain, on a regular basis? The thought of it is laughable! But I'm sure Moses had a pretty toned physique after all that hiking.

Moses needed that time with God, and he needed it to be alone. Leading millions of people isn't easy. (Shoot, leading *three* people isn't easy!) Leading millions of whiny, complaining people who just want to go back to Egypt *really* isn't easy. They say that leadership is lonely, and I imagine it truly was for Moses. And yet, what a friend we have in Jesus. What a friend Moses had in YHWH. Exodus 33:11 says that the LORD "used to speak to Moses face to face, as a man speaks to his friend." The LORD is faithful to provide exactly what we need. The mountain may have seemed lonely to many, but to Moses, it's where he met with his closest friend. It's where he received direction. Refreshment.

* * *

Like Moses, Jesus himself often snuck away to the mountain to meet with his Father. Often after a miracle or intense time of ministry, such as the feeding of the five thousand in Mark 6. Sometimes he invited his disciples (Mark 3:13), but most times he went alone. Even Jesus, God Incarnate, needed a little refreshment to the soul. A little solo time with his Father.

The personal relationships and the level of intimacy that both Moses and Jesus had with God only come from time alone with him. Community, while necessary, cannot replace a personal relationship with the Father. Listening to podcasts or sermons, though helpful, cannot replace sitting quietly in his presence, waiting for him to speak.

In a previous chapter I mentioned that I was afraid of failing to meet God's expectations of me. This fear often kept me from direct interaction with him, hanging my head low in his presence, which at times led to periods of stagnation in our relationship. It is hard to grow in friendship or intimacy with someone when you're afraid of being alone with them.

After all of our training participants left that November, I came face to face with the reality that I had few friends, no community, and honestly, no life outside of work. There were a few people that I had grown close to, but it wasn't like I was spending every evening with them. I spent many nights alone drawing in coffee shops, trying on clothes in Old Navy dressing rooms, or watching TV in my bedroom. God was inviting me to ascend the mountain, to be with him, and I was slowly and hesitantly dragging my feet to the top.

I knew I was called to enter into a new place of intimacy with the Father, but I was scared. Scared of what he might say to me, of what he might ask me to do. (In case you haven't caught on by now, I had a *lot* of fears to deal with. I'll get more into that later.) I made myself busy; I tried not to let myself feel lonely. And I wasted so much precious time.

On one of my first trips back to Kansas, I had dinner at the home of my dear friends, Lauren and David. A whole group of us were gathered around the table that evening, as was usually the case at their home, eating and laughing and enjoying ourselves. They have the kind of home that makes you instantly feel comfortable. We sat around the table for hours before everyone left at 10:30 pm, but I hung around to chat.

The three of us caught up for a bit. Then David, as he often does, launched into what the LORD had been teaching him, and the two of them shared how they had been experiencing God in new ways over the last year or so. It's one of my favorite things about these friends; I always leave their house having learned something new. Together they encouraged me, prayed for me, lifted me up before the LORD. We worshiped, and we listened. The word David kept emphasizing that night to me was intimacy. Intimacy with the Father. Everything, he said, would flow from this place. Especially my creativity, Lauren added. Without intimacy, nothing new could be born.

It was two in the morning before I left that night. Lauren prayed that our faces would glow as we left their prayer room, like Moses after meeting with God.

Intimacy with God changes us. Moses, after just catching a glimpse of the LORD's back (Exodus 33:23), spending forty days and nights fasting on the mountain, and receiving the second set of tablets (Exodus 34:28), literally came down the mountain glowing. "The skin of his face shone because he had been talking with God" (Exodus 34:29).

In a similar fashion, Jesus took Peter and James and John up a mountain, and there before their very eyes he began to glow. He transfigured. "His clothes became radiant, intensely white, as no one on earth could bleach him...And a voice came out of the cloud, 'This is my beloved Son; listen to him'" (Mark 9:3, 7).

There is something about the mountain and alone time with God that makes us shine a little brighter. What did the Father want to do in my life on this mountain? How was he planning on transforming me? What was I missing out on because I was afraid to meet with him?

Because I was afraid to be lonely and afraid to be alone? We will never know if we don't start climbing. It can be hard work, and lonely work at times, but the view is worth it and the company at the top is great. And maybe, just maybe, you'll come down with your face and your clothes shining; for "those who look to him are radiant, and their faces shall never be ashamed" (Psalm 34:5).

07

yes to surrender

My pastor's wife read aloud to the group of young adults gathered in the living room on Thursday night: "And now, just as you accepted Christ Jesus as your Lord, you must continue to follow him" (Colossians 2:6, NLT). It was my first time attending the young adult's group at my new church. There were about twelve of us circled up with mugs of tea and hot chocolate. Lisa paused from reading the Scripture and looked around at us, "Jesus is not only our Savior or our friend; Jesus is our Lord. Is he *your* Lord?"

She had us close our eyes and imagine our lives as a house with many rooms. Maybe our families and friends were in one room, our time perhaps in another. Down the hallway is a room full of dreams and future plans. You get the picture. She asked if there were any rooms we weren't allowing Jesus to enter? Or maybe just allowing him to pop his head through the door? Or were all our doors completely open, welcoming him to move in and rearrange and bring in new furniture and haul away some of the old if he wanted?

I stared at Lisa in disbelief as I thought about the note on my desk at work from that morning. I had been finishing up my morning devotions when a thought popped into my mind. I wrote it on a sticky note and stuck it to my computer monitor to think about later: "We must not simply make room for God. We must give him the entire room."

Was there a room I was not letting him into? *Is Jesus actually my Lord?* Those words, that question, rang in my ears over the next week. What did that even mean?

Lord. We hear this word a lot. I don't know your "go-to" name for Jesus or God, but I'm a frequent flyer when it comes to using "Lord." But if we're going to say it, it's probably a good idea to know what it actually means. Maybe you remember Vizzini from the movie *The Princess Bride*. He continues to use the word "inconceivable" again and again before Inigo Montoya finally steps in and tells him he's *pretty* sure he's not using that word correctly…I was a little bit like him, throwing around the word "Lord" often, and the Holy Spirit finally acted as my Inigo Montoya, challenging me on its definition.

In the Bible, you'll often see "LORD" written in small capital letters. This was an attempt to translate the Hebrew word YHWH (Yahweh), God's name, into English. John Mark Comer, in his book *God Has a Name* (which I highly recommend, by the way), explains why it is so hard to translate YHWH:

> For one, we don't actually know what the vowels are because they were never written down. Almost all Hebrew scholars think Yahweh is right, but honestly, it's still a best guess. But the main reason is that over time the Hebrews stopped saying the name of God out loud…Instead they would call him other names…the most common title was *Adonai*, a Hebrew word meaning "Lord." In the ancient Near East, that's what a servant would call his master, so they used that title for God.[2]

In summary: When you see "LORD" (all capitals) in the Scriptures, it's in reference to Yahweh. The Great I Am. When you see "lord" (all lowercase) it's usually in reference to a human master, and "Lord" (just a capital L) is typically talking about Jesus. Phew! Did you follow that?

Even though each of these three holds a different weight and a different connotation, the word remains the same: lord, master. And if you look in the dictionary for a definition, you'll see that lordship entails supreme power or rule. The king. The authority. The boss. Circling back to the question from earlier, is Jesus actually your Lord? Is he the boss? Does he actually hold the reins? Or are *you* the master of your life?

* * *

Every time I was alone with my thoughts for the next few weeks, I would think about Jesus' lordship and feel a little sick to my stomach. I was resisting. And I didn't like it. I needed to surrender something, but I felt something else kicking back within me.

I considered the "house" that Lisa had spoken of. I pictured a fairly spacious house, perhaps with a wraparound porch, doors open and welcoming, but there at the very end of the hallway was this one peculiar room with the door shut tightly. A room full of odds and ends that had been relocated from the kitchen and the bathroom and the living room.

I have these two contradictory urges that reside within me: first, I love buying things. I love new, shiny, clean journals and purses and shoes and pens and books and home decor. And clothes. Oh, that sweet feeling of wearing a new outfit for the first and second and third time. But, on the other hand, I also love getting rid of things. I love the look of a sparse and organized closet, clutter-free shelves, and simple living. It's a vicious cycle. I buy new things, I get rid of things, and then

I buy some more new things. Sometimes, though, instead of actually getting rid of things, I put them under my bed in a suitcase, and I just pretend they don't exist anymore. Unfortunately, pretending things don't exist anymore doesn't actually benefit anyone. Moving day comes, and you still have to lug out all of that stuff from the suitcases you haven't opened in months.

This particular room in my "house" was the place I had stored everything I needed to get rid of and was just pretending didn't exist anymore. Because getting rid of it altogether was just a little bit too hard. What if I needed those things again? What if I regretted moving on from them? God was at the door knocking, and I was pressed up against the door yelling, "Just a minute!" while nervously looking over my shoulder at the room, filled to bursting in every nook and cranny.

I wasn't really sure what God was going to do in there, and I didn't want to let him in. I was too afraid he'd come in with a big box with the word "DONATE" or, worse, "TRASH" scrawled across the side in thick, black marker. I imagined him picking up all my beloved treasures and just chucking them carelessly into the box, taping it up, and walking out.

Rest assured, my friend, that God isn't like that. Sure, he wants to do some rearranging in there. He might remove some stuff. But God isn't careless. God isn't lacking compassion for us. God isn't out to get us. God's goal isn't to make our lives worse. God is for us, not against us! Let me say it again: God is for us, not against us! One more time: *God is for you, not against you.*

God knows me personally. He isn't going to come into my room and start decorating with a big red comforter and pictures of race cars and paint my walls tan. God knows that the color red is pretty low on my list of favorite colors. He knows that I know nothing about cars and don't care to. He knows that I think brown walls are the ugliest. Maybe he'll decorate in ways that I never would have thought of, but it'll still be me. It'll still be Becky. It'll still have yellow and pink and cozy blankets and pillows and candles and a plant that's really easy to keep alive. He knows me. He created me, after all.

* * *

"I just want to be able to say yes to Jesus, no matter what. Without being a diva," I wrote in my journal one morning. I thought about all the things that God had asked me to do over the last year and a half or so. I had done them, but it wasn't easy. And I know nobody expected it to be easy; I'm sure God didn't even expect it to be easy for me. But I felt like it should at least be getting *easier*, shouldn't it? It was like I would hand over the car keys, but still expect Jesus to sit in the passenger seat. And when he tried to coax me out of the driver's seat, I'd act surprised and throw a fit, but give in eventually. But then we'd stop for gas or snacks, and he'd come back out to the car with a special treat, just for me (probably Doritos or maybe a chocolate donut), only to discover Becky in the driver's seat again! Over and over and over again.

As I meditated on this concept of lordship, I finally came to a conclusion that shocked me: I love control. I love to be in control of my life and my plans and my time and my future. I never thought I was a control freak; I'm a pretty chill person. Being laid-back is one of my favorite parts about myself, in fact. Admitting that I crave control felt like I was betraying myself. It seemed out of character.

I don't often feel the need to control others or be in charge all the time, but I am coming to terms with the fact that I desire to control outcomes. I want my life to end up a certain way, and I want others' opinions of me to be a certain way, too. And because I feel like I know what the end goal is, of course I know the best and fastest way to get there, right? And how dare anybody else tell me otherwise!

Surprise, surprise, that's not exactly how this all works. I think the only thing we can count on here on earth is that we do not know what is in store for us is these temporary lives. Sometimes God gives us a glimpse of where we're headed; sometimes he gives us a glimpse of how we'll get there. But often, it all comes down to trust and taking one step at a time.

Our friend Moses knew where he was taking the Israelites: the Promised Land, Canaan. But he had to trust the journey and the steps along the way. He couldn't just head straight there; that wasn't the map that God had laid out for them. The LORD *literally* led them by cloud and fire:

> Throughout all their journeys, whenever the cloud was taken up from over the tabernacle, the people of Israel would set out. But if the cloud was not taken up, then they did not set out till the day that it was taken up. For the cloud of the LORD was on the tabernacle by day, and fire was in it by night, in the sight of all the house of Israel throughout all their journeys (Exodus 40:36–38).

I would love to know what life is going to be like for me in my fifties. In my forties, thirties even. I think God, in his goodness towards me, has kept those things hidden because he knows I would try to blaze my own trail. I'd try to fast-track it. I don't have the patience of Moses, to trust the slow journey there. I've been all over the map in the last decade. And honestly, I'm not sure what all of this is unto. But I have come to peace with asking for direction for simply the next step, and not the next three or ten.

When I still lived in Kansas, I was on my way home from work one afternoon. I lived about a twenty-five-minute drive from the church and had to switch highways multiple times. From K96 to I135 to I235. There was often a lot of congestion merging from K96 to I135, so sometimes I'd jump off one exit early and take the residential streets a little further up and skip I135 altogether.

On this specific afternoon, I was cruising along K96 as usual. I was quickly approaching my short-cut exit, so I craned my neck to see if I should get off early or keep on going. As I looked ahead, trying to see what was before me, I nearly missed the brake lights on the car in front of me. I gasped and slammed on the brakes just in time. I slowly exhaled, thanking God for my safety.

I think about that moment often when I consider my future. God has challenged me to stop looking for shortcuts in life, to stop trying to look so far ahead to avoid any roadblocks, but to focus on what is right in front of me. To take the path before me, even if it means I'll be sitting still in traffic for a bit.

* * *

The New Testament tells us a story about a rich young ruler. He has everything he could ever dream of, he's wealthy, he knows the Scriptures. And yet, when he asks Jesus what he needed to do to inherit eternal life, despite his obedience in following the Ten Commandments, Jesus says, "One thing you still lack. Sell all that you have and distribute to the poor, and you will have treasure in heaven; and come, follow me" (Luke 18:22). That doesn't sound that hard, right? But, the ruler's response was that "he became very sad, for he was extremely rich" (18:23).

This passage isn't to say that rich people can't follow Jesus. But this young man's lord was not Jesus. His lord, his authority and his master was his wealth. I don't want my love of earthly things, whether it's material possessions or relationships or my job, to cause me to walk away from Jesus with my head hung low because I just can't follow him. I don't want to be enslaved to my love of funny television shows or my want to have cute clothes or even my desire to be married one day. While those things in good measure are not even necessarily sinful, they can slowly start to steal the throne without us even noticing. And if we're not careful, we can find ourselves on the throne, too.

It comes down to this: Who is lord of my life? Me or Jesus? What do I care about more? A life of "happiness" and being in control, or an eternity of joy spent with Jesus?

In Jesus' own words, "What will it profit a man if he gains the whole world and forfeits his soul?" (Matthew 16:26). It was time to let go, to let Jesus into that last room of comfort and desires I had been hoarding. I was visiting a church one Sunday and heard Pastor Mike Fornwald say, "I love the good things Jesus has given me, but I don't love them more than my Jesus." I don't know Mike personally, but I will always remember this, and my deepest prayer is that I, too, can say this in full truth. May I love Jesus more than my very life.

08

yes to asking for help

Perhaps you've heard or read the story of Lazarus. Perhaps you haven't. In either case, I'm going to give you a refresher on the story, so settle in and get cozy.

Lazarus was the brother of two sisters, Mary and Martha. This was a special family; the Gospels comment here and there about how much Jesus loved these three siblings. They were his friends. I know that we can all be friends with Jesus, but to think of Jesus having human peers during his life on earth, outside of the disciples even, makes him even more human to me. Just imagine Jesus knocking on their door, asking if Lazarus was home. They go out back and lounge under a tree, making jokes and laughing together, maybe throw a frisbee around for a bit. I love it.

One day, Jesus was out somewhere, doing some ministry with his disciples perhaps, when he got word that his buddy Lazarus was pretty sick. But rather than drop everything and head to Bethany, where Lazarus lived, Jesus decided to stay a few days longer where he was. Strange, yes, I agree.

A few days later, Jesus knew that Lazarus had died, and he finally decided they should head on over to Bethany and check things out. "When Jesus came, he found that Lazarus had already been in the tomb four days" (John 11:17). Lazarus was dead. Super dead. Jesus was too late.

Or was he?

* * *

A few months after moving to Abbotsford, I was sitting alone in my little prayer closet, when I sensed the LORD speaking to me. "We need to take those graveclothes off," I heard. I was immediately reminded of the greenhouse. It was a different picture this time, but the same message: there were some things I was hiding behind.

"I thought we'd already taken care of this," I muttered to God, and was immediately convicted that ignoring my problems was not, in fact, the same as "taking care of them."

Something you should know about me is that I'm a fairly independent person. I mentioned early on that I'm pretty private and an internal processor. It's hard for me to ask for help. It's hard for me to admit when I'm struggling. A lot of this comes down to pride and wanting to protect my reputation, but I also see now that for many years I was buried underneath a pretty heavy weight of shame.

Dr. Rob Reimer, in his book *Soul Care*, talks about shame in relation to feeling "unworthy, unlovable, vulnerable, or inadequate."[3] Shame is not the same as guilt. We feel guilt when we are convicted by the Holy Spirit for doing something wrong, and that leads us to repentance. But shame is incessant. Shame makes it hard for us to lift our faces to God. Shame makes it hard to speak up. No matter how many times you confess sin, a heaviness still lingers. Dr. Reimer goes on to describe toxic shame as "a sense that you are not lovable. That something is wrong with you."[4] The only way to break toxic shame, he says, is revelation from the Holy Spirit himself.

"Revelation" sounds like a weighty word, but I promise you, even the most average Joe can have a revelation from the Holy Spirit.

My definition of a revelation is an "aha!" moment. A moment where things just make sense even though they never have before. You just have to ask. Ask God to help you understand. Ask God to show you how loved you are. Ask God to reveal himself to you. And he will. Just keep asking.

I didn't want to invite anyone into my problems. I wanted to do this alone: just me and God. Inviting anyone else in seemed a little too crowded. A little too vulnerable.

* * *

So, back to Lazarus: everyone thought Jesus was too late. People probably stared at him and rolled their eyes at him when he showed up *four whole days* late. Thanks for showing up, Jesus. Finally, Jesus. But Jesus wasn't late. Jesus is never late. Jesus approached the tomb and ordered that the stone be taken away (John 11:39). He prayed to his Father, and then yelled into the tomb, "Lazarus, come out" (11:43). People surely thought that Jesus had lost his mind, but "the man who had died came out, his hands and feet bound with linen strips, and his face wrapped with a cloth" (11:44). And here's the line that I want you to pay close attention to: "Jesus said to *them*, 'Unbind him, and let him go'" (11:44, emphasis mine).

Jesus brought Lazarus back to life. It is Jesus who revives our lungs and makes dead bones to dance and brings revelation. But what I find so beautiful and fascinating and complex is that Jesus invites community into the work thereafter. Lazarus, as alive as he was, came out of the grave still wrapped in those graveclothes. His hands and his feet tied; his face wrapped up. And Jesus looked to the *community*, to those gathered around, to do the work of bringing about freedom.

Can we just stop and let that sink in?

As the church, as a body and community of believers, Jesus invites us into the freedom process. I am humbled and awed by this. Why would he entrust me to participate in such an important task? Salvation brings about new life, yet sometimes we act as if we're still dead, as if we're still slaves to sin and darkness, and we need the help of others to help us take off the old graveclothes in order to step into the fullness of freedom.

* * *

You know I'm a huge advocate for time on the mountain. Time in the greenhouse. Time alone in your prayer closet or your tent or your chair. Time alone, but with Jesus. If you never spent time alone with your spouse when you were dating, would you have ever decided to marry that person? (I can't really say, I'm not married yet, but I don't think so.) But if our entire lives were meant to be spent alone with Jesus, there'd be no need for the church. We're invited to live in community, too. We see that in the life of Jesus, he often went from being with people, to being alone, to being back with people, back to being alone…like the ebb and flow of the tide.

I took a closer look at these "graveclothes" that Jesus was so keen on me removing. I knew that this time I couldn't do it alone; I needed to invite someone to walk with me more closely. I needed to crawl out of my little prayer closet. To unwrap my hands and my feet and my face. I needed community.

To be completely honest, community in Abbotsford isn't what I thought it'd be, or what I'm used to. My friends back home are a little more spontaneous, a little less busy, and always up for a last-minute party. But, if Canada has taught me anything, it's how to have deep one-on-one friendships.

The parties may be less frequent in my circles here, the game nights with fewer faces around the table, but the friends I have made here in BC have proved themselves trustworthy. They have taught me how to be real, how to be honest when I'm struggling. They have prayed with me and for me. They have helped me unwrap my graveclothes.

*　*　*

One evening I finally decided it was time. I needed to talk to someone about all of this. I texted Jess and asked if we could meet to pray together. I had a lot on my mind and heart. This was perhaps the first time I had really laid everything out there. The first time confessing my sin to another person. The first time I invited someone in. I cried a lot. I basically read straight from my journal because I knew I would chicken out otherwise. I read out my fears and the areas I was struggling in and my need for control and how I just couldn't stop shopping all the time because I was bored and lonely. I told her how I was afraid that God would ask me to stay in Canada.

There was nothing "big" or "awful" or "shocking" that I told her. But sin is sin. And sin unconfessed can wreak a lot of havoc in our lives.

Jess, in her wisdom and grace, kept pointing me to Jesus in that hour. Inviting me to speak directly to him. Asking God to speak to me through her. Asking God to give me revelation. And together, the Holy Spirit helped us uncover two things I never knew about myself: I am an angry person and a grudge holder, and this can lead to unforgiveness in my heart.

If I was caught off guard by the realization that I love control, I can't even begin to describe how I felt about *this*! Me? Angry? Becky Spahr? The joyful girl? The fun girl? The chill girl? The girl who loves yellow? *Angry*? But there it was. A whole list of people who had hurt me that I just couldn't move on from. Rapid fire scene after scene playing through my mind of moments that still brought tears to my eyes. Memories from five, ten, fifteen years prior.

As she listened, Jess was able to point out a pattern in my life: I have often felt abandoned and rejected by people I respect, often by circumstances out of their control or by my unvoiced and unmet expectations. This led to anger and disappointment on my behalf, that I once again left unvoiced, and created hard ground where only bitterness could grow. Jess, knowing her part in taking off my graveclothes, immediately called me on it and invited me into repentance. She invited me to name each person and each memory out loud, forgive them, and bless them. Over and over again until I meant it.

The beautiful thing about being a graveclothes remover is that it's not all on you. It's something you do with Jesus. It's something you do with the "dead" person, as mortifying as that sounds. It's a group effort. Your job is to listen, to point people to Jesus, to help them hear what the Holy Spirit is saying, to rebuke and challenge when necessary, and to encourage. (Remember, revelation comes from the Holy Spirit!) My favorite thing about the LORD is that when he asks us to do something, he will provide the strength and the wisdom and the direction; we just have to listen and respond.

Asking for help isn't always easy (take it from me), but it often makes way for that "extra layer" of freedom, just like the community unwrapping Lazarus from his graveclothes. I remember leaving that prayer time relieved that I had shared, but unsure if anything had actually "happened." Sometimes you feel like a huge weight has been lifted off your shoulders, and honestly, sometimes you don't. But, that being said, when I flew home for Christmas a few weeks later and looked some of these people in the eye, I felt different. My heart was soft, no longer hard and bitter. I felt love and joy in their presence. I remember looking around the room one evening thinking, "Wow, do I really have to go back to Canada? I love these people." Something had definitely "happened" in my heart, thanks to Jesus, and thanks to my friend Jess listening to Jesus.

09

yes to staying

I think the whisper started in November, but it could have been earlier. I was in denial for a long time. It was there for months, camping out in the back of my mind, quiet but startling. At first it was just an annoyance, like a fruit fly floating around the kitchen, but as time went on, it demanded more and more of my attention. I remember multiple mornings driving to work, entering the roundabout by the mall, and suddenly there it was again: *What if God asked me to stay in Canada?*

I hated this question. I hated it because I did *not* want to stay in Canada. I had only been living in Abbotsford for three months, and already I was homesick and everything was harder than I thought it would be. I didn't have very many friends, it rained too much, and I always felt lost. But the question lingered.

I just wanted to go back to Kansas. I know people think that's weird. What's in Kansas? Nothing, for most people, especially if you didn't grow up there. But I had friends and family and white queso, and I didn't have to use a GPS there. In Kansas people didn't make fun of me for the way I said the word 'decal,' and loonies and toonies were just Saturday morning cartoons. I was sure when I left for Thailand that I would be back. And I was sure when I accepted the internship that it was impossible for me to stay in Abbotsford. But, the question remained. *What if God asked me to stay in Canada?*

By December, I was finally able to ignore the pesky little voice. I shoved it deep down in the depths of my brain, like the suitcases under my bed full of items I forgot I even owned. Time to time I'll open them up, shocked at the number of things I thought I donated to Goodwill that are still right there in my bedroom.

In January I participated in my church's annual 21 Days of Prayer and Fasting. I decided to pray about my future for the three weeks. By day two, the anxiety and the question started to creep back in, and I wrestled like a toddler throwing a temper tantrum, hands clamped tightly over my ears. I did not want to hear the answer to that question. So I just stopped praying.

* * *

For many people leaving is hard, but for me, staying is often the harder choice. Staying requires investment, hard work. Staying means you can't be flaky; it takes commitment. Staying in Canada would mean I'd likely encounter more loneliness. I would need to put effort into forming new relationships and keep putting myself out there. Staying sometimes takes endurance, like treading water, before you can get to a place of rest.

At the beginning of the book of Joshua, we read about the Israelites crossing the Jordan River. This time was a little bit different from the crossing of the Red Sea; in my opinion, this time required a little bit more faith. Everyone knew that God was going to do something big, but they had to trust that he would really come through. This time instead of parting the waters *before* the Israelites crossed over, God instructed Joshua that the waters would part only *after* the priests got in. They had to step out into the water, a step of faith, and then they had to stand there while everyone crossed over.

Now the priests bearing the ark of the covenant of the LORD stood firmly on dry ground in the midst of the Jordan, and all Israel was passing over on dry ground until all the nation finished passing over the Jordan...For the priests bearing the ark stood in the midst of the Jordan until everything was finished that the LORD commanded Joshua... (Joshua 3:17, 4:10, 11).

The priests didn't have a hard job, per se. They just had to stand there, and the waters would remain parted as long as they did. But they had to remain faithful. They had to wait until the very last person crossed over, and there were millions of people. I'm sure they got tired, looking around for a lawn chair to relieve some of the pain, shifting from right foot to left foot and back again. Yesterday I went to an event and had to sit down after just an hour of standing still. But the priests stayed standing. They stayed faithful.

I felt God invite me through this passage to stay faithful. To not check out early. To stay standing until the end of my time in Abbotsford. I had only been there three or four months, and I was already counting down the days until I could leave. I was looking for an easy out; I wanted to get out of the Jordan.

* * *

Mid-January, I found myself at the kitchen counter one morning, staring at the wall as if in a trance. I was perplexed, anxious, asking God if he was indeed asking me to stay in Abbotsford. I was tired of worrying about it. Tired of not knowing. And so I said out loud,

"God, I'm not sure if you are asking me to stay. But if you are, or if you do, I say yes."

I kept looking for a sign, something that would make God's voice clearer perhaps. In hindsight, I see now that I was looking for a sign that told me I could go home and was ignoring the signs that were telling me to stay. It's almost comical to go back and read my journals from that time. There were *so many* signs, friends.

In the book of 2 Kings, we find a story about a king named Jehu. Jehu did a lot of good; he actually completely wiped out Baal worship from Israel. And yet, despite his hard work, he did not completely turn away from sin; he held onto the golden calves from previous evil kings (2 Kings 10:28-29). Here's what I wrote in my journal after reading this story that January: "Is there something in my life, LORD, that is like a golden calf? I've turned from "Baal worship," but am I still holding onto something?"

I literally laughed out loud when I read this today; I was so blind! After all that I had gone through just months earlier, learning about surrender and Jesus as LORD, claiming to give up control, expressing my desire to truly follow Jesus and say yes to him, I was still holding onto my plans and my desire for comfort. So, yes, Becky, I would say there was a golden calf hanging around.

* * *

A lot of people have asked me how I know when God is calling me to do something. I think it can be different for everybody because God speaks to us in different ways. For some people, he uses songs or Scriptures, for some he gives a mental picture, for some he impresses a thought on our hearts. I would say God speaks to me in many ways, but I'm not always paying attention. But if it's really God, I'll usually begin to see or hear a similar theme over and over again, in songs and books and sermons.

When I was in Thailand, a friend texted me to tell me she had been praying for me, and she sent me a short little paragraph of encouragement. In that text, she used the word "bloom." A few days later, on my birthday, one of my teammates gave me a card that read, "Bloom where you are planted." One of my other teammates gave me a bouquet of flowers. A Thai friend gave me some mascara, and I am *not* joking when I tell you that her exact words were, "to make your eyelashes bloom." The word kept popping up over and over all day, and I couldn't deny that God was trying to tell me something. It was honestly one of the best birthdays I've ever had; I felt like God went out of his way to give me a gift.

Another indicator for me that God is speaking is if an idea or thought just won't leave my mind over a long period of time. For example, the question, *What if God asks me to stay in Canada?* The fact that this question would enter my thoughts at random times, and the fact that it kind of scared me, had to make me wonder if it was the Holy Spirit prompting me.

This is the point when you should invite someone else to help you discern, someone who is wise and can help you identify whether your thought lines up with Scripture and sounds like something God would say. But, I have to admit that I often procrastinate discernment in community way longer than I should, resulting in a lot of anxiety built up in my own soul and spirit.

A red flag that I am likely going *against* the will of God is when I catch myself continually trying to justify my actions to myself or others. If I feel the need to back up my decision or actions constantly, that tells me that I've perhaps made the wrong choice, and I'm making up excuses because I'm not feeling at peace. Overexplaining, in my experience, is usually an indication of guilt.

This is often the point when I ask God very specific questions and pay attention to how I feel in my spirit. Do I feel anxious, nauseous, excited, peaceful? For me personally, before I get to this step, I have to be at a place where I'm willing to hear the actual answer, not just the answer I'm hoping for. Going back to chapter three when I talked about deciding between Thailand and Peru, my question was specific and direct: "I can't be this person you've called me to be *and* go to Peru right now, can I?" And instantly, in my spirit, I felt a rush of confirmation and peace, even though I was saddened as well.

* * *

If you sneak a peek into my journal, the white one with the llamas on the cover, you will find the following entry written, only one week after the "golden calf" question:

I am falling apart. Again. It seems to be a common thing for me lately. Following Jesus is hard. I think Jesus is asking me to stay.

Oh, Jesus, I can't see the bigger picture, but I know you have a plan.

I had slept horribly the night before. Perhaps in part due to the coffee I drank at 8:00 pm, but to be honest, a late night coffee has never done me in like that before. I woke up almost every forty-five minutes, heart and mind racing. Something I had heard Pastor Mike Fornwald say two weeks earlier rang in my ears: "It would be *torment* to be a Christian and not follow Jesus."

Maybe you've heard the story of Jonah from the Old Testament. Jonah was a prophet, and God gave him very specific instruction: "'Arise, go to Nineveh, that great city, and call out against it, for their evil has come up before me.' But Jonah rose to flee to Tarshish from the presence of the LORD" (Jonah 1:2-3). God asks Jonah, or rather *commands* Jonah, to do one thing; and Jonah goes the opposite direction, literally. For this reason, and because we really don't get to read much background information on Jonah, the poor guy has a pretty rough reputation today. He's the disobedient and grumpy prophet.

The story goes on to describe how Jonah gets on a ship that encounters a horrible storm, and everyone figures out it's because Jonah is disobeying God; so, he asks them to throw him overboard. What I find intriguing here, and what changed my perspective of Jonah, is verse 9. Jonah tells everyone on the boat, "'I am a Hebrew, and I fear the LORD, the God of heaven, who made the sea and the dry land.'"

In the middle of outright disobedience, Jonah claims to fear the LORD. It's only natural for us to roll our eyes and think Jonah a hypocrite in this moment. But how many times have I done the same thing? Claimed to be a Jesus-follower, a God-fearer, even when I'm caught in the middle of an act of disobedience?

Disobedience doesn't disqualify us from being Jesus-followers, and praise God for that, but choosing disobedience does complicate things. Going against the will of God is exhausting, like swimming against the current (or the Red Sea). But our God is a God of second chances, of redemption, of grace. Jonah got a second chance; the

LORD sent a big fish to swallow up Jonah and actually save him. And Jonah then had an opportunity to go to Nineveh like God asked.

I had a choice to make. I could go home, back to Kansas, if I really wanted. But to live in that kind of defiance just didn't sound pleasant. It sure sounded like torment. Exhausting. And so I finally said yes to staying.

* * *

I have found that it's really hard to say yes to God when you don't actually trust him, as I mentioned in an earlier chapter. Did I actually believe that God had my best in mind? Did I actually believe that God is good? Did I actually believe that his plan was better than the one I had so carefully been crafting? How quickly we forget! Had I not just seen how faithful he was to me in Thailand?

You and I, we think life is all about us. And newsflash, it's not. It's about bringing glory to the Father. And something about me staying in Abbotsford was going to bring more glory to the Father than me moving back to Kansas. Even just typing that out in this very moment makes me feel like the wind has been knocked out of me all over again.

I have this sin problem called entitlement. And I'm willing to bet a few bucks that some of you have it, too. I didn't realize it until last year, but I have this mindset that when I obey God—especially when it's really hard—he owes me something in return. And for a long time, I think that was the motivation behind my obedience. If I do that for God, he'll do this for me. If I go to Thailand instead of Peru, he'll give me the best team. If I stay in Canada another year, he'll finally give me a soul mate (ha!).

What's disgusting about this perspective is that it seems to make obedience optional in our minds. Radical obedience has become rare, and is almost over-celebrated. When I decided to go to Thailand, so many people told me that I would receive a reward in heaven for making such a tough decision. And sure, maybe that's true; who am I to say? But do your kids really expect a reward *every single time* they clean their room when you ask? When I decided to stay in Abbotsford, not for one, but for two more years, it was really hard to understand why God would ask me to do that. But my mom put it so beautifully: "God is squeezing Becky out of herself to make more room for himself."

God asks us to do hard things, things we would never want to do, not because he is mean or manipulative, but because he knows the very best thing he could ever give us is more of himself. And the only way for us to receive more of him is to give away more and more of ourselves. John the Baptist said it well, "He must become greater; I must become less" (John 3:30, NIV).

10

yes to being uprooted

My first year in Abbotsford I lived in a house with a large span of greenhouses out back in which peppers grew. I loved to run out there in the spring; it was a mile and a quarter all the way around. When May rolled around, the weather was beautiful. The sun high and hot. Rosie, one of the dogs, would often join me on my workouts.

One evening, I set out on my jog, earbuds in, music loud. I can't remember what song was playing, but I know it was a worship song. As I ran along, avoiding dips in the dry terrain, I suddenly started to have a breakdown, rather unexpectedly. I had been struggling for about a month, feeling distant from God, angry at his silence. "Where are you!?" I yelled into the empty berry fields that sat on the other side of the fence. I ran hard, angry, before slowing to a stop at the edge of the greenhouses. I stood with my hands on my hips, and the sun was setting behind me as I fixed my sights on Mount Baker.

I wanted a word. I needed to hear something from God. Something fresh. Something to silence my doubt that he wasn't with me anymore. The sun peeked out from behind a cloud and sent a stream of sunshine into the field. I started to walk towards it, but then retreated behind the greenhouse and hid, afraid of being seen by the neighbors. And that's when it dawned on me. *I had to get out of the greenhouse.*

Let me remind you of the imaginary greenhouse, boarded up, filled with struggling plants and flowers just yearning for sunlight. I had done a lot of the work of "tearing down" those boards while I was in Thailand, but I thought I was done with it. Yet here I was, at an actual greenhouse, and "coincidentally" preparing to move elsewhere.

I've learned that what was grown in the greenhouse wasn't meant to stay hidden away in the greenhouse forever. Fruit and vegetables get picked and distributed, and other plants are often transplanted to the garden.

Get out of the greenhouse. It was time to do more than just tear down the wooden planks. It was time to completely uproot and move out. God had been growing me, protecting me, shielding me, and I was ready for the great outdoors. He knew I could withstand whatever storm would head my way.

* * *

Coincidentally (or not), around this same time, I was learning a lot about roots and weeds. Not necessarily literal roots and weeds (although I did a lot of garden blog reading), but metaphorical ones, i.e. sin. Just like a weed, should a sinful behavior not be taken care of at its root, it'll sneak right back up in the garden of life.

In all of my blog reading, I learned about a couple different kinds of weeds. First, there are flowering weeds. Some of these weeds can look beautiful among the other flowers in your garden, but unfortunately looks aren't everything. They rob resources from the other plants, slowly malnourishing them. There are also invasive plants, which spread quickly and take over. They are really hard to get rid of, and like flowering weeds, they're not necessarily ugly, but they harm, and even kill, the other plants around them.

Just yesterday I was on a walk around Fishtrap Creek here in Abbotsford. I saw signs here and there throughout the park, with the word "**KNOTWEED**" written in bold, capital letters across the top. There were photos of this weed, along with the words, "Knotweed is an invasive species" in bright red text along the top, and "Knotweed is incredibly difficult to control" along the bottom. The signs included facts about knotweed and how to get rid of it. It's hard. It takes literal *years* to eradicate the entire root system. Years.

That may seem like a long time just to get rid of a weed. Is it really worth it? It sounds easier to just let it move in and stay. But weeds kill. And if you don't take a weed out at the roots, it will always grow back, and usually stronger. Kelly Clarkson knew what she was talking about when she sang those words, "What doesn't kill you makes you stronger!"[5] And just like weeds in a garden, we have to carefully take out the sin in our lives at the root, or it will just spring up again.

The spring and summer of 2019 was a season of weeding. And man, some of those weeds were tough. My wise friend, George, once told me, "If you ever get the chance to weed, do it when the weeds are small. It's a lot easier. And when the soil gets really dry and is no longer wet, it's even harder to get the weeds up from the root." He was talking about his literal garden, having no idea how much this applied to the condition of my heart as well.

* * *

You know how when you're cleaning out your closet or your storage room or your garage, there's a moment when it looks like a tornado ripped through, and things are just everywhere? Boxes here, piles of junk over there, this and that strewn all about the entire house and yard? It looks the very same way when you're cleaning up your soul, too.

My friend Jess is passionate about "cleaning house." From time to time, we'll come together and lay everything out on the table, confessing our sin and our fears before each other and God, asking if there's anything hidden that needs to come to light. Sometimes it's a quick process, and sometimes it's not. And exhausting as it can be to feel like you're constantly staring at a pile of your bad habits and ugly behaviors and addictions and comfort sin patterns, it's essential to the process. You can't clean out your garage without looking at *everything*.

The process of being transplanted from the greenhouse to the garden felt arduous. Imagine a gardener uprooting every single plant he cared for, one by one, gently lifting it up to the sun, closing one eye and inspecting the roots. Should this one stay or go? Are the roots healthy? Is it a weed? This is what it felt like God was doing in my mind and heart and soul. My self-awareness was being heightened, and what I saw wasn't always pretty. It felt like all my garbage was being dragged out of the garage into the driveway for everyone to see.

* * *

One morning at work, I came out of a meeting when a coworker and dear friend asked if she could talk to me. Her demeanor was serious, and I nervously agreed, racking my brain wondering what this could be about. We sat across from each other in the prayer room, and she took a deep breath. I swallowed, lump in my throat, starting to feel a little anxious.

She began to slowly share about how she had been praying about how to have this conversation with me, as she felt hurt by the way I had been acting towards her the past few weeks. She told me a few specific instances and identified a few behaviors in me that were not pleasant. I was grieved. How could I not have known how I had been hurting my friend?

As uncomfortable as the conversation was for both of us, it was truly beautiful. We cried together, our friendship was restored, and I learned a lot that day. I drove home later that day and mulled the whole conversation over in my mind, still a little shocked if I'm honest. I never saw that moment coming. And yet, I was grateful.

As ignorant as it sounds, that was the moment I realized that other people know that I'm not perfect. I've always strived to be liked and friendly and kind. And I am those things, most of the time I think, but I'm not *perfect*. I do things that hurt or annoy people, and I don't even realize. I've always known it, but I've rarely been confronted about it.

That day I saw that I really need Jesus to help me love people well. I can't do it without him.

***

I've read the parable of the sower a few times in the last week. If you haven't heard it before, you can find it in Mark 4. I'm going to be really transparent here and tell you that I often tune out during this story. I've heard it so many times. It seems overdone, really. How many different ways can you possibly interpret this story? Jesus explains the meaning pretty clearly. For once, we don't have to take a fine-toothed pick to it to figure it out.

But something about it struck me a little differently this week. Particularly in Jesus' explanation of the parable. The parable itself is about a sower who goes out to scatter seed. I picture him just walking along, scooping up handfuls of seed from a bucket, tossing it here and there while listening to a podcast. Some of it falls on the path, some on the rocky ground, some among the thorns, and some on good soil. Naturally, only the seed sown in good soil will produce grain. This takes us to Jesus' explanation to his disciples in Mark 4:14–20:

> The sower sows the word. And these are the ones along the path, where the word is sown: when they hear, Satan immediately comes and takes away the word that is sown in them. And these are the ones sown on rocky ground: the ones who, when they hear the word, immediately receive it with joy. And they have no root in themselves, but endure for a while; then, when tribulation or persecution arises on account of the word, immediately they fall away. And others are the ones sown among thorns. They are those who hear the word, but the cares of the world and the deceitfulness of riches and the desires for other things enter in and choke the word, and it proves unfruitful. But those that were sown on the good soil are the ones who hear the word and accept it and bear fruit, thirtyfold and sixtyfold and a hundredfold.

I never really took the time to think about the first three "soil conditions." Because I'm a Christian, and have been for two decades, I've just always assumed I fell under the fourth category: good soil. But, that season of uprooting was revealing that not all the soil of my heart was in tip-top condition.

As we talked about already in chapter two, good soil is the key to a healthy garden. If your garden isn't thriving, the soil is a good place to start investigating. Fortunately, gardeners actually have the ability to improve and enrich the condition of their soil. They can add organic matter or compost, they can get some worms in there to add nutrients the natural way, they can get it tested to see what's missing; the list goes on.

And I truly believe that the Gardener of our hearts does the same thing with us. Parts of my heart were a little rocky; in some areas, I definitely lacked good, strong roots. And parts of my heart had been overtaken by thorns; I had a lot of other desires that I struggled laying down for years. But if we stick with Jesus, even in the seasons of uncomfortable weeding and uprooting and tilling, the soil of our hearts will be all the better for it.

* * *

At the end of July, I literally moved from the home with the greenhouses into the townhouse where I currently live. We had a garden off to the side where my roommates were growing kale and carrots and beans and tomatoes. Nothing is quite like eating a salad that you literally grew and harvested yourself. Oh, what joy our Father must feel when the fruit of our lives brings him glory.

This year, I got to watch one of my roommates plant the garden. In early spring, she bought compost to enrich the soil. It smelled horrible, but it's what the ground needed. Weeks later, she carefully raked the soil and plotted out where she would plant everything. She carefully placed the kale and lettuce and broccoli seeds in straight lines, using twine to mark out what was what.

It wasn't the right time to plant everything, though. Almost a month later, she finally brought out the tomato and pepper plants and nestled them next to the beans. I watched in wonder; how did she know when to plant what? How did she know how to do all of this? She knows when to water, when to harvest, and how to prepare what she's harvested. I have no gardening experience whatsoever, and I'm glad she doesn't expect me to do anything except water when I'm asked. And yet, I'm welcome to eat whatever I want.

Our Gardener, likewise, knows what he is doing. He knows when to plant and water and harvest. He knows the difference between weeds and vegetables, even though sometimes we can't even tell ourselves. He invites us to join him, guiding us with careful instruction, teaching us how to water and how to identify weeds. And together we get to enjoy the fruit of our labor.

11
yes to dying

It was July 1. Canada Day. I was fasting to regain vision and focus. I was nervous about the pending status of my work permit. The next two years of my life were dependent on this one thing. I had agreed to stay in BC for two more years, purely out of obedience to God, and I knew that the acceptance of my visa extension would be the final affirmation that I had heard him correctly.

Transitions in our organization just a month earlier made staying even harder for me to swallow. That day in July, I prayed an honest prayer:

> *Today, although everything in me wants to ask for my work permit to be denied, more than that, Jesus, I want to trust you.*
>
> *In November, my prayer was that you would not only be my Savior, but that you'd also be Lord of my life. Through all of this, I've been learning to make you Lord over all. When I said yes to you in 1999, I said yes to whatever life you would want to give me, whether that's in Kansas or here in Canada.*
>
> *Jesus, may I remember that my joy is not dependent on circumstance. But I don't want to hide anything from you either. I WANT TO GO HOME. I lay it all out before you,*

and I'm going to stay if you say the word. You are faithful. Even when I don't get what I want.

A few hours later, I ran out to get gas. It was golden hour, and as I drove down the hill to the gas station and slowed around the curve, my attention was drawn to a car stopped on the side of the road with its hazards on. I drove a little further and then saw it: a deer on the road, writhing and thrashing around, clearly in immense pain. The deer could barely stand, yet it tried so desperately to resist going down. Up and down, up and down. Limbs flailing. Two young men stood there and took videos on their phones. The driver of the car was calling someone. I was disturbed, yet I drove on.

I filled my tank with gas and drove back the way I had come. The deer had passed in those few minutes. Someone had gently placed a sheet over its body and was crouched down next to it. The boys with their phones were gone.

I replayed the scene over and over again as I pulled into the driveway. "Okay, LORD," I said. "I'm fasting today. Surely this means something for me." I sat in my car for a minute as I realized that *this* is what I had looked like the last eight months.

In Christian circles, we often use the phrase "die to self." It's a bit of a challenging concept to wrap our brains around, but I love the way Dr. D. W. Extrand summarizes it:

> When someone "spiritually dies to self," self ceases to exist – that is, SELF IS NO LONGER THE REASON FOR ONE'S EXISTENCE. As such, the individual is no longer concerned with "his own will or happiness," because he is no longer in the picture...he is no longer the center of his

own little universe...he no longer continues to arrange the world around himself.⁶

I had been trying to die to myself. I was trying my best to surrender the steering wheel, the keys, and the driver's seat. I was even asking God to help me do it. But I was resisting at the same time. Up and down, up and down. Limbs flailing. Just like that dying deer.

I half laughed, half cringed, apologizing to God for subjecting him to watch such an agonizing scene for so long. Immediately I was comforted though, knowing that in this particular scenario, God was not watching me with his phone out to take a video; this wasn't entertainment or amusement for him. He was patiently and gently letting me wrestle it out, and he would be there to take care of me at the end.

Today as I write this, it's been exactly one year since I saw that deer. It feels like an eternity ago, and yet, just like yesterday at the same time. I can see it so vividly in my mind. This morning I spent some time reflecting on the last six months and wrote out some of the things I've learned. At the bottom of the page, in all capital letters, underlined, I wrote, "<u>I FEEL SO ALIVE</u>."

One year ago, I was in such a different place. I felt like I was dying, and yet, I knew I wasn't dead yet. Part of me still wanted life to be all about me. It was a slow suffering. The president of the organization I work for once said that if you're resisting God's call on your life, you aren't dead yet. Last year, I was resisting. I was flailing. I was anxious and worried and stressed.

Like the deer, I was reluctant to die to self, and it took me way longer than it should have. I was afraid of never being happy again, of never being comfortable again. Afraid that it wouldn't be worth it. But what I failed to realize a year ago is that dying to self doesn't actually mean that you stay dead. We die to our sin and our worldly selves *so that* we may become alive in Christ.

* * *

I remember learning a verse at camp in sixth grade. That was the year we got light blue T-shirts, and I got to room with my two best friends. We recited this verse multiple times a day and probably got cool prizes. I memorized it in a different translation, but in the ESV it says, "I appeal to you therefore, brothers, by the mercies of God, to present your bodies as a living sacrifice, holy and acceptable to God, which is your spiritual worship. Do not be conformed to this world, but be transformed by the renewal of your mind" (Romans 12:1–2). Notice Paul says *living* sacrifice, because we'll come back to that.

Before Jesus came to earth and sacrificed himself on behalf of all mankind, the people of God used to have to make animal sacrifices in atonement for their sin. In other words, they would kill an animal to make up for not being perfect. It sounds a little crazy, I know, especially if you're an animal rights activist. But, this was how the people of God could keep a holy status with their Maker.

Holiness is important to God because he deeply desires to be with us. To walk and live and dwell among us. But God cannot be in the presence of sin; the sacrifices were the way to wipe the slate clean. A priest would make these sacrifices on an altar on behalf of the people. In Exodus (yep, we're back to my favorite book of the Bible again!), the LORD gives Moses very specific instructions regarding the altar and all of the sacrifices. And as he's telling Moses about the priests and the altar, he says, "Whatever touches the altar shall become holy" (29:37).

I know what you're thinking, "Cool, Becky, but get to the point. I don't get where you're going with this."

Okay, okay, so going back to Romans. We're supposed to offer ourselves as sacrifices. We're supposed to crawl up on that altar and lay it all down. Surrender. Die. But it does not end there! We are *living* sacrifices: we don't stay dead. And when we touch that altar, we are made *holy*.

Don't believe me? Check out the Scriptures: "[God], even when we were dead in our trespasses, made us alive together with Christ...and raised us up with him in the heavenly places in Christ Jesus" (Ephesians 2:5-6).

Paul tells us "to put off your old self, which belongs to your former manner of life and is corrupt through deceitful desires, and to be renewed in the spirit of your minds, and to put on the new self, created after the likeness of God in true righteousness and holiness" (Ephesians 4:22-24).

And we read this in Romans: "We were buried therefore with him by baptism into death, in order that, just as Christ was raised from the dead by the glory of the Father, we too might walk in newness of life. For if we have been united with him in a death like his, we shall certainly be united with him in a resurrection like his. We know that our old self was crucified with him in order that the body of sin might be brought to nothing, so that we would no longer be enslaved to sin...Now if we have died with Christ, we believe that we will also live with him" (Romans 6:4-6, 8).

I think I always imagined death to self like my entire self just slipping away into the abyss, and then Jesus would come and inhabit my empty body or something. But Jesus doesn't want us dead; he just wants our lives to be all about him.

***

Around the same time as the deer incident, I was reading the book *Sick of Me* by Whitney Capps with some friends. Highly recommend. I remember each week I would come to our discussions having discovered that nothing is about me. My *life* isn't about me, my *salvation* isn't about me, and not even my *suffering* is about me. I just wanted *something* to be about me! But, it's not. Nothing is about me. Not even my birthday.

I've always loved birthdays. I love to celebrate, and I love to make other people feel special. But, because I feel like I always go out of my way to celebrate others, I'm often let down on my own birthday. I have very high expectations. It's one of the things I like least about myself. It's the one day of the year when my extreme selfishness is put on display for all to see.

For one birthday while I was in college, I think number 21, my expectations were severely unmet. It was a Wednesday, and I had youth group in the evening, followed by our student-led worship night. I was feeling down when I arrived at the church, and playing games with a bunch of middle schoolers didn't help much. On top of that, nobody wanted to go to worship night with me when I got back to campus.

I walked alone in the dark to the historic chapel as I mumbled a quick prayer of repentance. I knew that this day was just as much about Jesus as every other day was. My birthday didn't give me an excuse to act like a brat or be selfish or short with others. I just wanted to feel special.

That night, in the old, low-lit chapel, I worshiped with my hands high and my eyes squeezed shut, and it was like I met the joy of Jesus face to face. I felt the tangible presence of the LORD, and I knew he wanted me to feel special on my birthday, too. Because even though life isn't about me, our God still loves me and cares for me and loves when I'm filled with joy.

After worship, I went over to the cafeteria for some late-night tater tots with two of my guy friends. A girl who was on the worship team approached our table and paused. "I looked over at you three worshiping tonight and could just sense the presence of Jesus. It was as if a radiant light was bursting out of your faces!" When our lives are about Jesus, other people notice; and it brings him glory.

* * *

July turned into August, and August turned into September. The leaves started falling. Dying. I started to feel anxious all the time. I was at work one morning and felt sick to my stomach, but I knew it was spiritual, not physical. I rolled my chair over to my friend's desk and asked her if she could pray with me. We went out back and took a little walk around the building as I expressed my recent feelings to her. It was as if I could physically feel the presence of fear, and I wasn't even sure what I was afraid of. She and I took a seat on the curb to pray.

We had barely even bowed our heads when, out of nowhere, a hearse drove up. Like, you know, the big black cars that transport coffins…coffins with dead people inside of them. It pulled right up to us and parked, I kid you not, two feet away. I stared at my friend and then at the driver. We kind of laughed as we stood up and moved to a different spot. But I couldn't get that image out of my head.

A few weeks later, I was still thinking about it. And, as morbid as it sounds, I was picturing myself lying inside that coffin in the back. "Well, here we are, God. I'm dead. What more do you want from me?"

I gave up my dreams and my plans, and it felt like the life was sucked right out of me. I was the walking dead.

But, God isn't looking for a bunch of zombies to roam the earth. The *resurrection life* is waiting for us on the other side of dying to self. Death brings about new life! Just look at nature: who else just loves all the changing leaves in fall? Do you ever think about how all those leaves are actually dying? And there will be a season of dormancy after, but spring is coming. New life is coming. John 12:24-26 says,

> I tell you the truth, unless a kernel of wheat is planted in the soil and dies, it remains alone. But its death will produce many new kernels—a plentiful harvest of new lives. Those who love their life in this world will lose it. Those who care nothing for their life in this world will keep it for eternity. Anyone who wants to serve me must follow me, because my servants must be where I am. And the Father will honor anyone who serves me.

Fruitfulness is impossible without death. When we try to hold onto our own ways of living, we just end up lonely. A kernel of wheat doesn't die for nothing; it dies to produce new life! But it has to be pushed down deep into the dirt first. And it's really dark down there.

12

yes in the darkness

I've always been a fairly positive person. Maybe that comes with having unknowingly numbed the majority of my emotions at an early age. Grandma died when I was young, but I was old enough to remember the sadness I felt and never want to experience it again. Before you go all therapist on me, I'm working on it, okay? Back to positivity. Call me what you will: cheerful, jovial, jolly. But I wouldn't dare call myself peppy or even enthusiastic. I have found that most people, though, use the word "joyful" when describing me. (Also see: laid-back. And, my personal favorite, funny.) I've just always had something within me that makes me feel "light."

A cheesy quote that you might find cross-stitched on a pillow at your aunt's house says, "There is sunshine in my soul today." I relate to that on an embarrassingly deep level. If I ever take up cross-stitching, my nieces will find this pillow on my couch, no doubt. There's just something about the sun, about a clear sky, that brings utmost joy to my being. I love the light.

That being said, most of my life, I had a difficult time relating to and empathizing with the weary, downtrodden, anxious, depressed, and melancholy. I just didn't get it. Just...be happy. Just push through. Isn't that how it works? Sure, I've had my share of cloudy days here and there. Even the *sun* has cloudy days. But I've always managed to bounce back rather quickly.

Until I couldn't. Until it seemed like the clouds had suffocated the sunshine, and all that was left was darkness. Darkness moved in, and she brought a lot of baggage, along with few friends she so kindly invited: fear, anxiety, and shame.

I've always known that the level of my productivity is directly related to the environment around me. My work ethic has always taken a dip in the fall and winter, when the sun sets early and rises late. The alarm clock goes off, I turn towards the window, and my whole being groans into the dark. In the spring and summer, I couldn't care less about sleep. Work and play all day; I'm here for it. I know someone who won the title "boy who dances with the sun" in his high school yearbook. I'd like to have that title. (But the girl version.) The sun and the blue sky bring these bones to life unlike anything else out there in the world. I knew that moving to moody British Columbia would take its toll on me, but this was something different. This wasn't a darkness that Vitamin D could fix.

This, I believe, is what St. John of the Cross called "the dark night of the soul." And what a long, dark night it was.

* * *

It was a normal evening for me in the early fall. My "normal" in those days was not everyone else's "normal." I was preparing for twenty-one students from around the world to arrive the next afternoon for another two months of intensive discipleship training, which would once again require my undivided attention for eight weeks straight.

On top of trying to figure out how to die to self, I had been struggling off and on with a lot of big faith questions for the last five months or so, the aftermath of a conference focused on digging up the junk in our souls. As someone who lived much of her life ignoring conflict, pain, and any feeling that provoked sadness, perhaps the amount of fear and brokenness in my life that was brought to light was a little too much for me to handle in such a short amount of time. I walked away from that conference heavy, a little bewildered, and, in my own words at the time, "needing to know I'm not crazy and that this Jesus-thing is real."

I felt like that conference broke me. It was like the tiny pebble hitting the windshield; what started as just a nick in the glass would soon spiderweb and completely shatter my entire perspective. I started waking up in the middle of the night and having these really odd, out-of-nowhere, dark fears and thoughts about God. It was as if my fear of the dark from childhood came back—the nights when I used to think something was in the house, and lie awake, eyes squished shut, unable to move.

As a child, I had read in the Gospels about how "Satan entered Judas, called Iscariot, one of the Twelve" (Luke 22:3). The Twelve, here, is referring to Jesus' disciples...his best friends. They went everywhere with him. Learning from him, doing miracles with him, praying and eating and drinking and definitely having fun with him. Judas was one of the twelve. And he betrayed Jesus...his friend. I always thought that if Judas, one of Jesus' best friends, could do that...is it possible that I too would betray my Jesus one day? Did Judas have a choice in this? Or was his fate as the Betrayer of Jesus predestined and sealed? *What did that mean for me?*

I never doubted God being real, but I doubted my ability to stay faithful to Him. Doubted the sincerity and realness of my faith. Doubted that I was *actually a Christian.* Doubted the security of my salvation.

It was as a young preteen that I developed what I often refer to now as "Judas Iscariot Syndrome." Symptoms include fear of betraying Jesus, being unsure of salvation, or just plain faking one's friendship with Jesus. The last time I could recall suffering from this evil disease, which I now know is a lie straight from the mouth of the devil himself, was at age nineteen. But here I was again, seven years later, a seemingly completely different person—a leader in ministry, even—lying in my bed in the middle of the night, crippled under the crushing weight of fear.

* * *

Fast-forward about three weeks. Something started stirring in my soul. Something that, honestly, didn't feel great. It felt a lot like conviction. And when the Holy Spirit convicts this girl, he pokes real hard, right in the gut. I went to a trusted friend in tears, and we got on our knees to pray. It was there that I confessed aloud that I was afraid of the Holy Spirit and what he might ask of me, and therefore, I had started to quench his voice and movement in my life.

I won't go into great detail about what happened next, because that day was incredibly personal and moving for me—and something I want to keep between Jesus and me. I will say, though, that I encountered the Holy Spirit in a new way on the floor of the apartment that afternoon, and I believe that the Lord was equipping me with strength and weapons for what was to come over the months ahead. I wish that I had realized it sooner.

The next week brought highs and lows. I experienced beautiful times with Jesus and the community around me, but also times when fear started to creep into my heart and mind, leaving me unsettled and grumpy. I tried to explain it to a friend as I invited her to pray with me one afternoon. "I just feel...darkness," I told her. "Physical darkness. Physical fear, right here in the middle of my stomach. And it won't go away."

Many days I found myself thinking about the famous line from the book of Ecclesiastes, "Everything is meaningless." I was tired. Unsettled. Not wanting to engage in deep or spiritual conversations because they made me anxious. Being in God's presence, being in silence, and sometimes being in worship made me anxious. What was going on? Was I missing something?

I was truly on some kind of faith-crisis rollercoaster, or so it seemed. I could be completely up one morning, sure of the truths found in Scripture, only to find myself in the pit of despair just a few hours later.

I tried hard to remind myself of what I know to be true:
- I know the Holy Spirit resides in me.
- I know I am saved.
- I know God is with me.
- I know He loves me.
- And I know that following Jesus is a *choice* more than a *feeling*. I cannot change my heart, but Jesus can. I can simply continue to say YES and move forward. So I say yes, Jesus. I say yes.

* * *

I wanted so desperately to pack up and go home. To say I couldn't do it anymore. To suppress the feelings, to numb myself by watching hours and hours of television or napping while listening to loud music. But I couldn't do that this time.

I went through many moments in the middle of the dark when I didn't even recognize myself. Who was this girl? I was afraid constantly. I didn't want to talk or even be around my friends. Easily irritated, annoyed, avoided people. I guarded my time with a suspicious eye, not wanting to interact with others, and yet, I was afraid of being alone. I felt no motivation to invest in those around me. To love them well. I carefully constructed a mask to hide behind though. I had a reputation. I was obsessed with self, yet sick of self at the same time.

I liked the old me. The joyful, carefree me. Why did I have to change? Why did I have to be sanctified? I remembered the words of Jeremiah 18:4, "And the vessel he was making of clay was spoiled in the potter's hand, and he reworked it into another vessel, as it seemed good to the potter to do." I am the clay. I am the vessel. He is the potter. Who cares if the old pot was half decent? Nice, even? Dare I say, beautiful? The pot he is re-forming me into will be better. It seems good to him, even if it may not seem good to me at the time. Did I really believe this?

Would I continue to faithfully serve, faithfully praise, and faithfully obey God, even in a season of quiet and darkness?

Would I choose to believe the truth that He will never leave nor forsake me? Or will I let my changing circumstances and feelings dictate my truth? Truth is truth. It can't be changed.

A few months earlier, I had felt a gentle whisper from the LORD say, "Ignoring things doesn't make them go away." I couldn't ignore the fear this time; I couldn't pretend the anxiety wasn't there. As much as I hated feeling sad and down, I had to force myself to camp out in the dark. To not run away. To wait. To invite the Lord into the mess with me.

* * *

I was tired. So tired. Tired of fighting for my mind. Tired of not being in control of my thoughts. Tired of forcing myself to believe. Tired of the battle. Tired of the persistent lies. Tired of getting beat up. I didn't know what to do. I remember one afternoon I was just baking an apple crisp in the kitchen when it hit; I stood still, frozen in my thoughts, the feeling of fear slowly creeping up on me.

I wish I had the words to describe what it feels like. The quite literal weight of fear on my soul. The fear of being afraid. Driving home after work with anxiety building up in my chest, dreading going to sleep that night. Knowing the minute I turned off the lights, the lies would begin their attack.

I knew I had authority in Christ's name, but I was afraid. I was afraid of what I would find, of what would happen. Afraid that maybe God wouldn't actually show up for me.

A year earlier my team from work and I witnessed and experienced a pretty intense spiritual battle with one of our students. Her story of freedom isn't mine to tell, but know that it's beautiful and inspiring and real. And her story changed me.

It took me nearly a year to realize how large of an impact this experience had on me. Much of this moment went unprocessed, resulting in a large amount of fear that I hadn't dealt with, hadn't shared with anyone. So I ignored it, pushed it away, pretended it hadn't happened.

There's a story in Mark 5 that pierces my heart every time. Jesus and his disciples head over to a new area on the other side of the sea. Right away, they encounter a man with demons. It sounds like something from the movies, but these demons gave him super strength. People tried to lock him up with chains and shackles, but he could break out, no problem. The text says that "night and day among the tombs and on the mountains he was always crying out and cutting himself with stones" (5:5). But then. He encounters Jesus.

Jesus commands the many demons out of him and into the herd of pigs nearby (that's another thought to ponder for ya). And the man is fine. He puts on clothes, takes a seat, acts completely normal. And the people watching? Well, the people are terrified. *They beg Jesus to leave.* Not exactly the reaction you would expect, right? Why aren't they celebrating this man's freedom?

They were afraid of the power of Jesus, afraid of change, even afraid of freedom. Even when it's so good. I hate that I identify with these people.

I read this passage one morning and knew that I had to change. Knew I had to lean into the power of Jesus. Knew I needed freedom.

I didn't want to be the person who asked Jesus to leave.

I realized that this was not going to go away on its own. And it wasn't going to happen overnight. I had to choose to keep trusting Jesus. To choose to choose Jesus. To choose to choose joy. To choose obedience. To hold on to his promises.

If I didn't start taking my freedom seriously, nothing would change. And isn't that the definition of insanity? To continue doing the same thing, over and over, while expecting different results? If I actually wanted to see different fruit in my life, I had to *change*. If I wanted to go to bed at night without feeling afraid, I needed to change something.

> *Becky, this is a daily battle.*
> *A daily fight.*
> *You keep choosing temporary peace over the everlasting.*
> *You choose quick fixes over the long-haul process.*

Becky. Train with me. Fight WITH me. We're in this together. Cling to me with everything you are. I KNOW you're tired. One day at a time.

the space between

between the former
and the future
lies a shadow
slowly creeping
into my soul
like the evening tide.

a shadow once feared
has become
a blanket,
a covering,
a meeting place,
the hiding place
from which I can see
His goodness pass before me,
knowing His promises
shall too come to pass.

faithfully I cling
in the shadows
to the One who is faithful.

13

yes when I'm afraid

Here's the thing about darkness: darkness demands a lot of attention. It's hard to see much in the dark; it takes focus. It's hard to see your own hand in front of your face, not to mention the people around you. And the darkness is loud. Not loud in a yelling kind of way, but loud in a confusing kind of way. There are lots of whispers in the dark—whispers that are hard to identify if you've never taken much time to get to know the voice(s). And most of those voices whisper lies. But it's hard to know what's a lie when there are so many of them, and if you aren't really sure what's truth.

So there you are in the dark, turning and twisting, trying to find the familiar Voice amongst the whispers. Squinting your eyes to try to see a little better, to try to find even the faintest little spark of light. But most days, it's just too much work, so you just look down or close your eyes and let everyone talk at once, wishing you knew how to not listen.

It was Sunday morning, and I was in church, but not in my usual seat. I sat alone, a little closer to the back on this particular morning. We stood and started to sing praises, and I felt the anxiety rush to my chest. I grimaced as I fought to keep singing.

It's hard to sing when there's a whisper telling you not to believe the words. It's hard to declare truth when you're not sure if you mean it. I was tired of feeling like I was faking it.

That morning, though, as I mouthed the words of a familiar worship song, I realized I had a choice to make. I could continue to focus on the fear, letting it capture all of my attention, my thoughts, and my energy. I could dwell on the "what if's" and the evil things. Or, I could choose faith and focus on sweet Jesus. Fear or faith, Becky? Fear? Or faith? The choice was really up to me.

Being able to name your fears, I think, is one of the most powerful ways to break their hold on you. The experience I mentioned earlier of our student's intense spiritual battle, while beautiful and inspiring, sowed a tiny fear in my life that had grown over the year. And I ignored it, hoping it would go away on its own. It slowly gnawed at my soul, eating away at my steady demeanor. I took a sideways glance at it now and then, not really sure what it was, but too afraid to look it in the face, just the way Satan likes it.

That morning in church, I boldly looked fear in the face, demanding it to show itself. And I was a little surprised by what I saw.

I had spent the last year of my life consumed with fears around spiritual warfare and the demonic, and that fear was probably more powerful than a demon itself would have been. I spent a year being afraid, being silent, being focused on nothing but my fear, which in turn, fed its power. The enemy is full of deceit, a true master of illusion and tricks of the light. "What if" is the flint he uses to light up a raging fear-fire inside of me, and with that, he was able to convince me to keep my eyes fixed on fear over faith. So many times, I came before the LORD and begged him to show me anything inside me that was not of him. I cleared the space. I made room for him to show me. And yet, I was motivated by the fears of "what ifs" rather than the faith that the Holy Spirit would be gracious enough to show me.

It was then that I realized how important it is to know the truth found in Scripture. Right there, right in Romans 8, it says, "For I am convinced that neither death nor life, neither angels nor demons...nor anything else in all creation, will be able to separate us from the love of God that is in Christ Jesus our Lord" (8:38-39). I could quote this verse, but I didn't live by this verse. I wasn't walking in this truth before.

Not even a stupid demon can separate me from Jesus. I know that now. I live that now.

*　*　*

When I was a kid, I often heard and used the phrase, "If you believe in Jesus in your heart..." I don't know that it was ever really explained to me, but my interpretation of this phrase alone seriously shaped my definition of faith, and not necessarily in the healthiest way.

My biggest obstacle to overcome in my time of darkness was fear and shame that I didn't "believe enough." That because I was struggling with some doubt, because I had been feeling distant from God, because I didn't understand everything, because I felt anxious about God-things, I didn't actually "believe in my heart." Somewhere along the way, I picked up the idea that my feelings were an indicator of truth. I thought that believing in my heart was equated with "feeling God," so when I woke up one morning, and then another, and then another, feeling his absence, I started to panic. Did I not believe anymore? This caused a vicious cycle of trying to make myself "feel God," resulting in disappointment when I didn't feel any different, causing shame for not believing enough, and around again.

Here's the deal. Faith is a lot like love. Some days you "feel it" and some days you don't. But just because I don't *feel* love for my friends or family or coworkers on a particular day doesn't mean I don't love them. And it doesn't mean that I'm a bad person either. It means that I'm human. I can make a choice whether to love them or not.

Likewise, some days I feel on fire for chasing God-things. I want to be in his presence; I want to share with others; I want to praise his name. Some days I want to stay in bed and watch movies and fill my body with junk food. On both days, I have a choice to make. I can choose to pursue Christ, or I can choose to pursue desires of the flesh.

Faith isn't a feeling; it's a choice.

No matter how I *feel*, the truth about Jesus doesn't change. The truth about who I am in Christ doesn't change. I've said it before, and I'll say it again: *truth is truth.*

Sit on that for a bit. I'll wait.

* * *

To constantly feel on edge all the time and not know why is simply exhausting. I had experienced some low-level anxiety before, and even some instances of fairly high levels (hello, Peru vs. Thailand 2017). But all of those times, I knew what I was anxious about, most of them involving a major life decision. If you're into the whole enneagram craze, I'm a classic nine. Making decisions is hard for me, especially when they affect other people (and they always do). This time was different, though, in that I had no idea what was triggering my anxious thoughts. As I look back, I can see that I always lived with great fear, ever since I was a young child. I made a list of everything that I can remember ever being afraid of in my whole life. And the list was long.

Most of those fears were triggered by very hypothetical situations that I took to be more serious than my mother ever intended:

Mom: If the doorbell rings and you're home alone, don't answer.
My brain: It could be a robber or a murderer or a kidnapper.

Mom: If you get home late, park in the driveway instead of the street.
My brain: So nobody can kidnap me before I get to the front door.

Mom: If there's a fire in the hallway, climb out your window.
My brain: The fire will probably start while I'm in the bathroom where there aren't any windows. (And then someone will kidnap me!)

And although most of these childhood fears were quite comical (for instance, if Santa could come down my chimney, why couldn't a burglar?), those small and silly things planted seeds that grew into bigger and more serious fears over time. And, as I'm learning, ignoring things doesn't make them go away. In fact, ignoring a weed is the worst thing you can do. And fear is a nasty, nasty weed.

I met a girl that fall who had surprisingly been experiencing something very similar to what I was going through. And she didn't tell anyone either, not for over a year. She sometimes struggled to worship or read her Bible or to be around other believers, just like me. She felt guilt and shame over feeling this way, which kept her silent. But one night, she came forward and prayed with a friend, and she was set free. No more fear, no more shame.

Hearing her story sent a shock wave through me. I would never have guessed what this girl was feeling. Likewise, this was exactly how I was feeling, and nobody really knew.

And it dawned on me for perhaps the first time that I, too, could be set free.

The night that I heard her story, I realized that I had believed the lie that I would live in fear for my entire life. Maybe not at the intensity it had been the last few months, but it had never even crossed my mind that I could be completely set free. I didn't have to just learn how to cope with this fear. I could live *without* this fear.

I had to stop being so passive about my freedom. About this fear. I needed to actually press through to Jesus—not just to a little comfort or relief. I remembered that hearse driving up to me behind the church. Once again, I saw myself lying dead in the coffin in the back. I had died to myself, but I hadn't taken up my new life. I hadn't yet stepped into the beautiful, wild, powerful journey Jesus has set before me. I was just lying there in the coffin, clinging tightly to all of the things that Jesus had put to death, asking when it was all going to be over.

* * *

Halloween night was the worst it had ever been. I had a great day (hyped up on all that sugar), but then I got into bed, and the fear set in. Bad. I couldn't sleep. I laid there and wept before finally texting two friends after midnight, asking them to pray for me. I quoted Psalm 23 over and over before finally drifting off to sleep.

As I drove to the grocery store a few days later, I felt like Jesus was telling me to keep fighting. I was in the thick of the forest. Things were hard. This was a hard season full of hard lessons to learn, and walking through the dark and the storm is HARD. But we can have hope. The breakthrough will come. God is with us, even if He feels far off. He's not walking out on us.

Still, I wrestled with a conflicting thought: when am I supposed to fight, and when am I supposed to let the LORD fight for me?

But then it clicked. I have to be disciplined in keeping still and fixing my eyes on Jesus in order for Him to fight for me. I must not sit by passively and just *expect* Him to fight. I must sit in His presence, still, asking Him to fight. I need to take action. I need to change. To stop being passive.

I need to know God more. And I need to ask for help. It's so hard though, because the enemy wants to keep me silent. It's part of his tactic with me, and it's worked in the past.

I think the enemy knows who I am. Just like God does. The enemy sees the fullness of the Becky I was intended to be, the same way God does (you know, minus the love and wanting what's best for me and stuff). And in a weird way, that's encouraging. The enemy sees what I'm actually capable of, and he tries to distract and destroy because he knows that once I really know who I am, I'll be a whole lot more dangerous.

I was starting to understand.

I may be a broken hot mess most of the time. Maybe you can relate. But Jesus can, and will, make us whole again. I'd attributed these thoughts, fears, and lies to so many things—the weather, the time change, loneliness, God wanting to teach me something...and maybe the physical did have something to do with it.

But. But God would never bind someone. He would never leave me in chains and bondage to teach me a lesson. He doesn't stand there dangling the key in front of me, taunting me. The LORD, YAHWEH, this God is about freedom.

I had been thinking that God was the one causing me to doubt and fear and experience darkness. And that's wrong. That's a lie. That is the enemy warping the image of God.

The enemy is up to evil. No good. He's lying, and he's distorting truth, and God IS GOING TO MAKE GOOD COME from this BECAUSE THAT'S WHAT HE DOES, AND THAT'S WHO HE IS.

Evil happens. And the LORD takes that situation and says, "Hhmm, let's take this and that from here and this over there, and make this beautiful thing." And voila! He is an artist. Every circumstance will yield good fruit for those who love him. He doesn't make bad things happen and then put a good spin on it. God uses all things for his Glory and our good. Even this fear that the enemy was trying to drown me in; God will use this for good. For encouraging others, for building my character and my stamina, for battle training.

Father, you see my frustration and my pain and my confusion and my tears. And you do not take this lightly. You do not laugh; you are not waiting on the other side of the darkness, impatiently tapping your watch, eyebrows furrowed, yelling for me to hurry up. No. You, Father, you are gentle and kind. "As long as it takes," you say, as you take my hand and lead me on.

I couldn't do this alone. I decided that day that this paralytic was getting up from the poolside, and she was calling some friends to carry her up to the roof, cut a hole in it, and take her to Jesus. I wasn't going to lie there helpless any longer.

* * *

A few nights later I woke up at 3:30am and was awake for an hour. And guess what? I was not afraid. I had good God thoughts. I even had some worship tunes in my brain. I could taste the victory. It was so close.

I felt like I was entering the war so differently than times before. I felt peace. Confidence. I knew, really knew, that the victory belongs to Jesus. I didn't feel like I was doing this in desperation to feel better or "get fixed." This time, I knew God had more for me than hiding in my bed afraid at night.

A few days before I was scheduled to meet, pray, and battle with some friends, I read Deuteronomy 20:3-4:

> Hear, O Israel, today you are drawing near for battle against your enemies: let not your heart faint. Do not fear or panic or be in dread of them, for the LORD your God is he who goes with you to fight for you against your enemies, to give you the victory.

I don't feel like I have to explain why these verses still bring tears to my eyes.

As I read this, I pictured a really intense battle scene. Take your pick of any ancient war movie: long-bearded, burly men on horseback, swords in hand, arrows flying through the air. And there I was at the back kneeling. The Father put a shield up around me and charged forward on his horse. I needed only to be still and wait.

This battle rages on all the time. But we need not be distracted. He sets a table for me in the presence of my enemies. Come to the table. Dine without fear of what's going on all around.

And when it feels like he's far or distant, it's because he's at the front lines, fighting for you.

14

yes to eye contact

One of the hardest things to do when you're intimidated by someone is maintain eye contact with them. I know this because I really value looking people straight in the eye when they're talking. And I perhaps keep eye contact for a little longer than most people are used to, especially with strangers. It's not so long that it makes people uncomfortable (unlike Steve Martin's character in the movie *Baby Mama*), but long enough to communicate, "I see you, and I'm here."

This is a habit I was unaware of until I moved to Canada, and I'm still not sure if it's just a Becky thing, or if it's a Midwest thing. When I first moved to Abbotsford, nearly every time I went out in public, people would start conversations with me. Strange, unsolicited conversations.

One woman told me it was her birthday and her family was out of town, so she was going on a shopping spree and rented herself a hotel room. A businessman wanted to know all about salted caramel mochas. Another woman in the cookie aisle told me all about her weight loss journey, and a man interrupted us to tell us the Neapolitan ice cream is the best ice cream ever if, and only if, you put equal parts in a bowl and mix it together.

There was also the elderly man who told me I looked beautiful "most days," and he would personally tell my boyfriend to propose to me sooner rather than later. I didn't have a boyfriend. Oh, oh, don't forget the man in the gray suit who quickly came to my rescue so that I didn't waste my money on organic broccoli. And the apologetic man who almost bumped into me, who lost his wife of 18 years last November.

I always asked myself, and others, why? Why me? Why do these strangers feel the need to tell me these very odd details about themselves?

I like to look at people. In their faces. One particular day, I went by Great Canadian Superstore after work, and it was bumpin'. The line was long, and our cashier was stressed out. I was two people back, but I looked at her and waited for her to see me. I smiled at her. *One-Mississippi, two-Mississippi.* She launched into telling me all about her stressful day and what she was going to do after work. *Aha*, I thought to myself. *It's all in the eyes.*

* * *

Coming, and staying, out of the darkness required me to fight to keep my eyes on Jesus instead of fear. To make eye contact with him instead of staring at my problems. God is continuously inviting us to fix our eyes on what we can't see. Instead of being fixated on what we know and the situation around us, we need to fix our eyes upward. It's hard to do sometimes; it's like trying to tear your gaze away from a horrific car wreck. You don't want to look, but you can't stop.

In late November, I met with two dear friends of mine to go to battle against the fear. We prayed, we rebuked the devil, we read Scripture, we worshiped. I confessed my fears and pleaded with God. I talked to God, they talked to God on my behalf, and we told the devil he was *not* welcome.

I wish I could say that I woke up feeling peace and completely different the next morning. But, I didn't. That night I had trouble falling asleep again.

But this time I refused to lose hope. I knew my God would bring me through this. I would fight with Him. I needed to be on my knees as He fought on the front lines. That's where I felt called to be. I started changing my habits. I began each morning in silence just listening, inviting the Holy Spirit to invade, to strengthen me. To teach me how to lock eyes with Jesus even in the middle of challenging circumstances. This life will always have hardship, but it's also true that we will always have Jesus.

Each morning as I sat and waited, my fear slowly dissipated. I started to feel more like myself. I started falling back in love with Jesus and looking forward to time with him instead of fearing it. I was reminded of his love for me, reminded of his constant pursuit of my heart. It was like each morning a little layer of fear was peeled back and thrown in the garbage.

One evening, a friend was praying for me and had a picture in her mind of me with wooden legs. She said God was giving me new legs. Wooden legs. He was taking me somewhere new that only these special wooden legs could take me. And although the legs were new, the foundation wasn't. He was teaching me how to walk on those new legs right then.

As I prayed into this more, I thought about why someone would even have wooden legs in the first place. The only logical explanation would be amputation after some kind of injury. (Although, in the modern world, carbon fiber prosthetics are more likely). My legs felt pretty damaged after the season I went through; I will likely always walk with a limp even with the new ones, but that limp will serve as a reminder of what has been conquered. I don't walk by fear anymore. I have to walk by faith—*these* are my new legs! Fear has been cut off in Jesus' name!

* * *

Choosing to live differently takes a lot of work, especially when the external doesn't change. We're creatures of habit. I wake up every morning at the same time to the same alarm tone. I put on the same old, worn-out llama slippers (even though I bought new ones last Christmas) and drag myself to the bathroom to put on the same makeup I've been wearing for years. I sit in the same seat at the kitchen table every morning as I sip coffee with hazelnut creamer out of the same mug.

I'm not a scientist or a doctor, nor will I pretend to know anything about the mechanisms of the human brain, but I can't help but think that if our external habits, routines, and patterns are so deeply ingrained within us, how much more so are our thought patterns?

I went to a small Christian college in rural Kansas. All underclassmen had to live in the "quad" on campus—old (like, *really* old) dorms that formed a square. Behind the girl's quad were the upperclassmen townhouses—around twelve townhouses in a long straight line, with a sidewalk forming a rectangle out front.

Now, if you ever took geometry in school, you'll remember that the hypotenuse (the longest side of a triangle) is actually the shortest distance between two points. So do you think students ever actually walked on the sidewalk? No, we forged our own path, corner to corner. Maintenance tried and tried to keep us off the grass, but it was no use. A path had been worn, and by the end of our senior year, maintenance gave in; a new sidewalk was poured.

When you are used to one way of thinking your entire life, what do you think the paths look like in your brain? Are the maintenance guys yelling at the stray thoughts to keep off the grass? Or have they already given in and started pouring that new sidewalk? Do you even have maintenance guys up there? Or do you let your thoughts walk anywhere they want to?

I have a small team of maintenance employees at work in my mind; they wear orange vests and they try to act tough, but they have the reputation of being lazy people pleasers. And man, when those fear thoughts started walking wherever they wanted to, maintenance didn't give a whole lot of pushback. They shrugged their shoulders, looked at each other and thought, "Hmm, these guys look familiar. I've seen them walk here before!" And they started mixing concrete.

I didn't know that I was actually responsible for my thought life. I didn't know I was the boss of the guys in the orange vests. I didn't know I could tell thoughts where to walk, or to leave the premises immediately. I thought my brain controlled me, not the other way around. I was so used to thinking fear thoughts and to looking at my problems that I just thought that's how things were and always would be.

***

In the Old Testament in the book of Haggai, the first chapter is about rebuilding the temple. It talks about everyone being concerned about building their own homes to look really grand and beautiful and paneled, while the temple is in ruins.

For much of my time in BC, I became much too consumed with building my own kingdom while the Kingdom of God sat in ruins around me. But eventually I grew tired of everything being about me and my comfort and my desires. I was constantly in a state of being stuck in my own head, lost in thought, thinking about why I was unhappy and how I could fix it. It was like my eyeballs were facing the wrong way; instead of looking outward, they faced inward.

To look at Jesus requires getting out of our own heads.

Psalm 27:8 is one of my favorite verses: "You have said, 'Seek my face.' My heart says to you, 'Your face, Lord, do I seek.'"

I used to be afraid of seeking his face, I think. I was afraid of the look he would be giving me when I finally found it. Afraid that he'd be frowning, or that his eyebrows would be furrowed, or worse—when I finally found his face and met his eyes with mine, he wouldn't even look back at me.

In the book of Genesis, we find a story about a woman named Hagar. She was an Egyptian servant of Abram and Sarai. Sarai was barren, meaning she couldn't get pregnant, but God had promised Sarai and Abram a child. So, like many of us do, Sarai took matters into her own hands: she told Abram to get Hagar pregnant. I think Sarai's plan was for Hagar to be the first surrogate mother. But I guess she didn't think that through all the way, and Sarai ended up being really jealous of Hagar because of the child she bore Abram.

Hagar fled to the wilderness because Sarai was such a jerk to her. And the text says that "the angel of the LORD found her by a spring of water in the wilderness" (Genesis 16:7). I love that it says he *found* her; he was looking for her. He noticed her missing, and set out in search of her. The angel goes on to make some promises to Hagar that are a little confusing, but she's honored. And in response, the Bible says that "she called the name of the LORD who spoke to her, 'You are a God of seeing,' for she said, 'Truly here I have seen him who looks after me'" (16:13).

Our God is a God who sees. He does not hide his face from us. Sometimes it may be hard to see in the dark, but when you put in the work, you *will* find his face. And the more you work to find his face, the easier it will be to find it each and every time.

In *Blue Like Jazz*, author Donald Miller starts his book by painting a beautiful word picture about Jesus walking toward him on a dirt road. "Years ago He was a swinging speck in the distance; now He is close enough I can hear His singing. Soon I will see the lines on His face."[7]

It's hard to see someone's face when your back is toward them, or when you're really far away. As we live life with Jesus, that journey brings us closer. We walk alongside him, hand in hand. We sit across the table and dine together, candles lit between us, illuminating the smiles on our faces. Run to him, walk with him, sit beside him. We start to see the wrinkles around his eyes from smiling.

* * *

Have you ever seen a bald eagle out in the wild? It is breathtaking, every single time. When I first moved to British Columbia, I knew bald eagles lived here, but I rarely saw them. Now I know that it's because I just wasn't looking.

In the spring, I started walking and running more. Like, almost every day. As did the rest of the world, thanks to COVID-19. On my walks, I would often admire the tall trees. I love the forest here. I'm a Kansas girl, and the trees there are few and far between. Nothing like BC. Naturally, because the trees are so tall, my eyes would wander up toward the sky. That's how I started to notice the eagles.

One morning in early April, I was journaling at the breakfast table while I sipped on my hot coffee with hazelnut creamer. I casually glanced out the back sliding door and audibly gasped. I flung off the blanket I had wrapped around me and nearly spilled my coffee as I ran to the window. There, in the tree right behind our house, a majestic bald eagle sat perched on a branch.

I stood and watched in awe for almost five minutes, until he finally spread his wings and flew straight towards the house, swooping up and over the roof. I returned to my chair, sitting in silence, amazed. I turned back to my journal and asked God if he was trying to tell me something. I had seen *so* many eagles in the last month; what did they mean?

Over the next couple of days I did a little bit of internet research and talked to a coworker who has a First Nations heritage. I couldn't shake the feeling that God was trying to speak to me through all of these eagle sightings. I saw more eagles that spring than I had in my entire life.

My coworker told me that he believed the eagle was a symbol of prayer, as they fly higher than any other bird and are closest to the Creator. They are a messenger of sorts, mingling with us down below and then soaring high above the clouds in the heavenlies. Kind of like Jesus, maybe—in that he was both man and God. He dwelt among us on earth, and yet sits enthroned in heaven. I read online that eagles, in Christian art, are often used to symbolize Jesus' resurrection. An eagle taking off in flight is a powerful image, and its wings even look a bit like the cross.

Not long after, I received word of a tragedy back home: a friend's brother had passed away. I was angry and sad and confused, and so I set out for a hard run. I ran and ran, like never before, and I prayed out loud as I went, huffing and puffing. As I neared the end of my four-mile run, worship music pumping loud, sweat running down my back, I saw it: a bald eagle, swooping down into the field and then back up, landing in a nearby tree. I laughed and thanked God out loud, knowing that he was near. He was here. God with us.

These days whenever I go out to walk or run, or even drive, I have found that my eyes are glued to the sky, scanning and searching for the beautiful sight of a bald eagle. I used to run with my head down, staring at the ground. It was too discouraging for me to see how far away the finish line was! But now, Jesus is literally training me to fix my eyes upwards. He is reminding me of his presence and nearness. Of resurrection life. To pray. That he hears me. To look up instead of down. To make eye contact with him, long enough to see him smile.

15

yes to standing firm

Have you ever watched the show *Arthur* on PBS Kids? It was my favorite show for way too long. Like, until sixth or seventh grade. Every day after school I would race home, pour myself a bowl of Goldfish crackers (in an empty margarine container, to be specific), and flip to channel 8. If you've ever watched the show, you'd know that there were two short episodes with a brief intermission in the middle, "A Word from Us Kids."

One particular segment kept me up at night: the one with the earthquake. I don't remember much, except for footage of kids talking about an earthquake at their school. I can still see one scene vividly in my mind of a girl lying on a bathroom floor, holding onto the pipes underneath the sink for dear life. That itself was enough to haunt me for years.

It wasn't until a few weeks after seeing this episode for the first time, when little wide-eyed, fearful Becky wandered upstairs in the middle of the night, and my mom reassured me we didn't get earthquakes in Kansas, that my fear of my home or school collapsing into the earth subsided. And even now that Kansas *has* actually experienced some earthquakes (what is happening!?), I can still easily convince myself, "Everything's fine; we don't get earthquakes in Kansas."

There's a short teaching from Jesus in Luke 6 about how to build your home so it won't collapse:

> Why do you call me "Lord, Lord," and not do what I tell you? Everyone who comes to me and hears my words and does them, I will show you what he is like: he is like a man building a house, who dug deep and laid the foundation on the rock. And when a flood arose, the stream broke against that house and could not shake it, because it had been well built. But the one who hears and does not do them is like a man who built a house on the ground without a foundation. When the stream broke against it, immediately it fell, and the ruin of that house was great (Luke 6:46-49).

When I read this passage, I think of the horrible floods in Oklahoma that happened a couple of years ago. I saw photos of water literally up to the roofs of some buildings. Just looking out your bedroom window would be like being in a submarine. I remember seeing footage on the news of a house that, at first glance, appeared to be built right on a river. Then I realized that it was a street, a very flooded street, with brown, muddy water gushing at outrageous speeds. The house was barely hanging on, and finally just let go. Down the "river" it went. Completely taken out. I wonder what condition the foundation was in before the flood?

Before you buy a house, the foundation is one of the (if not *the*) most important things to have inspected. You want a house with a strong foundation because the entire structure relies on it to remain standing. If your foundation has cracks, you're bound to have a plethora of problems. Your entire house could collapse, like the one Jesus talks about.

When I was in my darkest season, I came to the realization that foundation really *is* everything. The storm came, and I wanted to give up so many times. But because I had built everything—my entire life—upon the truth that Jesus is real and Jesus is King, I couldn't just walk away. I definitely had some cracks in my foundation; some days, I could feel the ground shake beneath me and the water rush in on all sides. Sometimes it seemed like Satan would knock me off the Rock. Those were the times when I found it absolutely essential to remind myself of the Truth.

We see in Luke 6 that a few things are involved in building a strong foundation: coming to Jesus, hearing his words, obeying him, and digging deep. Laying your foundation on the rock doesn't happen overnight; it happens by actually spending time with Jesus. Come to him. Sit at his feet. Read his Word, learn his voice, and listen to what he has to say. But we aren't supposed to just hear the words. We're supposed to obey! Actually do what he asks us to do. Choose to say yes! Solid foundations are not shallow; we have to do some work and take the time to dig. Dig deep. What do you need to sift and sort through in order to find the solid rock?

***

Just about one month before I "entered the darkness," I was doodling in my journal and drew a little stick figure of myself standing on top of a rock. I wrote "truth" on the rock, and asked Jesus to help me to stand firm, humming a few lines of the old hymn, "On Christ the Solid Rock I Stand" as I drew. I was entering a busy season at work and knew I would need the strength of Jesus to get through it.

One week later, a colleague and I were praying together. He told me that he saw a picture (in his mind) of me standing on top of a very rounded rock, and Jesus was behind me, slowly lifting up my hands. I smiled widely and quickly flipped through my journal, showing him what I had drawn just days before. He stared at the picture and then at me, mouth agape. "That's exactly what I saw," he told me, shocked.

Standing on the rock, standing on truth, is of utter importance when undergoing attacks of the enemy. If we don't know the truth about who Jesus is and who we are, we can be easily swayed by the lies of the enemy. If we aren't convinced that Jesus is King, someone or something else can easily take over the throne in our hearts.

During one particular moment in that dark season when I was just making breakfast and listening to a podcast, I suddenly realized that we just can't really know much truth outside of God. People change. Circumstances change. Science seems to change even. But God? Jesus? The Holy Spirit? ALWAYS. THE. SAME. The truths about YAHWEH are indeed Truths, with a capital T!

***

Steadfast and faithful,
Never changing.
Always here,
I AM.

Shaky and flaky,
Always searching.
Ever-wandering,
I am.

***

In Ephesians 6, Paul describes what we call the Armor of God. This passage (verses 10-20) talks about different parts of a suit of armor: the belt of truth, the breastplate of righteousness, shoes of the gospel of peace, the shield of faith, the helmet of salvation, and the sword of the Spirit. What's interesting to me in this description of the armor is that Paul talks very little about fighting, but rather focuses on *standing*.

Verse 11 says to "put on the whole armor of God, that you may be able to *stand* against the schemes of the devil" (emphasis mine). Verse 13 says, again, to "take up the whole armor of God, that you may be able to with*stand* in the evil day, and having done all, to *stand* firm." Paul doesn't say to put on the armor so that we can fight; he says to put on the armor so that we can stand.

We know that the two typical responses to an attack or fearful situation are either *fight* or *flight*. Paul calls us to something else here, though: standing firm. We don't exhaust ourselves by fighting (a battle that's already been won, by the way), nor do we take ourselves out by running away. We stand firm to the end, confident in knowing that even though things are hard right now, we have to stick to our guns because Jesus will fight for us, and Jesus always wins. But Paul says that we need to put on the *whole armor*, all six pieces, to do so.

1. The **belt of truth** is the first piece mentioned. Belts keep our pants up so we don't trip over them and fall. Knowing the truth does the same. Remind yourself of who God is and who you are. Search the Scriptures for verses and passages that declare truth about the character of God, Jesus, and the Holy Spirit. In the same way, remind yourself who God says you are as his child.

2. Next, Paul lists the **breastplate of righteousness**. Breastplates protect the heart. How do you know if your heart is right? Start with a simple prayer from Scripture: "Search me, O God, and know my heart! Try me and know my thoughts! And see if there be any grievous way in me, and lead me in the way everlasting!" (Psalm 139:23-24). Ask the Holy Spirit to reveal anything within you that displeases God.
3. **Shoes fitted with the readiness of the gospel of peace** come next. Shoes really bring an outfit together, don't they? In BC, most people take their shoes off before they enter someone's house. I remember going to a bridal shower during my first month or so here, and I was dismayed to find out I had to take off my kicks at the door. My outfit just wasn't the same without them. Likewise, armor without shoes is lacking. And our faith without actually knowing the gospel (the good news) and the peace it brings is lacking, too.
4. Paul says the **shield of faith** extinguishes "all the flaming darts of the evil one" (v. 16). Have the faith to continue standing when the enemy attacks; have the faith to believe God is fighting on your behalf. Having faith that God will do what he says he'll do is enough in itself to scare the devil silly.
5. Am I the only one who hates wearing a helmet? Unfortunately, in both the physical and the metaphorical sense, I seem to often leave my helmet behind…The **helmet of salvation** protects our minds from the lies and deceit of the enemy. Protect your mind, keep a tight rein on your thought life, and think about things that are true, honorable, just, pure, and lovely (Philippians 4:8).
6. Last, but certainly not least, is the only weapon listed: the **sword of the Spirit**, which is the word of God (Ephesians 6:7). Know. Your. Scriptures. I can't emphasize this enough. More and more

often today, I meet young Christians who don't know the Bible. The Bible is the window to God's heart! How will you know his character and what is true if you aren't reading his holy Word?

I say all of this because learning to stand, and being willing to stay standing even when my legs started to ache, was necessary to get out of the dark. So many times, I wanted to just sit and wallow in sadness and loneliness. So many times, I did. I am like the hostess with the mostest when it comes to pity parties! But you know who loves pity parties even more than I do? Satan.

I knew in my mind what I had to do and what I believe; I just actually had to stand up and do it. But I wasn't doing it. Not until a friend told me to my face that I had a choice, and I needed to start doing something about it. I needed to suit up in the *whole* armor so that I could stand.

* * *

A few months after coming out of this dark season, I was reading in the Psalms when I came across the first three verses in chapter 40, and I thought my heart was going to explode:

> I waited patiently for the LORD;
>   he inclined to me and heard my cry.
> He drew me up from the pit of destruction,
>   out of the miry bog,
> and set my feet upon a rock,
>   making my steps secure.
> He put a new song in my mouth,
>   a song of praise to our God.

> Many will see and fear,
> and put their trust in the LORD.

I couldn't have summed that season up better myself; thanks, David. And my deepest prayer is that the story of how God rescued me from that pit and put my feet on the rock would cause others to put their trust in the LORD, too. That this season, this story, would encourage the hearts of those of you who are walking through the dark; that you would know that light is coming. God will hear your cries, and he will put a new song in your mouth. For "this I know, that God is for me" (Psalm 56:9).

16
yes to coming close

I haven't really dated much, just here and there. There have been a few blind dates, a few dates that were never discussed again (were they really dates? I'm still not sure), and a few first dates that weren't too bad. But very, very rarely second, third, or fourth dates (did I mention that was rare?). Oh, the woes of being a single twentysomething in this generation. Dating is hard.

I've been asked out a few times by strangers, and those are usually an obvious no. I was at the mall with some students from our training program once, when a guy came up out of nowhere, told me he thought I was cute, and sat down next to me in the food court. He was so confident that I thought I surely had to have met him before. But no, he was indeed a complete stranger. And he actually had the guts to invite me out to coffee in front of five other people! That's bold.

I sat next to a guy on a plane once who was every girl's dream. He was so smooth that I didn't know if he was flirting with me or just being nice when he offered to give me a tour of Vancouver sometime. He was very cute, and we both were playing the game *Bejeweled* (if you've ever flown with me, you know that game is my favorite travel companion); but he invited me to a party that *started* at 10:00 pm; that was enough of a red flag for me that I pumped the brakes on that one.

If I'm honest, though, I think I look for reasons to reject guys because I'm scared. I'm scared that if I don't reject them first, they'll eventually reject me. It took me a long time to get to the root of it, but this fear of rejection is the root of *most* of my junk. It's why I'm afraid to try new things, why I don't talk a lot about myself unless asked, why I choose to sit on the sidelines instead of play the game. I call this "self-disqualification," and it's a habit I'm trying to break.

I can come up with an excuse for anything: "Well, I'm American, so..." or "I live in Canada right now actually, so..." "I'm only here for three years, and..." "Oh I'm actually only part-time..." "I don't really go here, but..." "I have no idea what I'm doing..." You get the idea.

What took me even longer to figure out, though, is that I do this in my relationship with God, too. I mentioned it before in chapter four: I have lived in fear that I won't meet God's expectations for me and that he'll reject me for it. The more God knows about me, the closer we get, the more reason he has to reject me. I know cognitively that it doesn't work like that, but my heart is slower to understand.

* * *

In the last three years, I've noticed a theme of God calling me into deeper intimacy with him. Person after person after person has given me words or verses or pictures of Jesus inviting me to come closer. To see him as the true Bridegroom. I get it, already. (But, do I really?) And yet, the words keep coming. Just last week someone spoke the same thing over me. I'm clearly not there yet.

In December, someone I know gave me a bit of a rebuke: She said I long for connection with others, but I'm good at walking on stilts. Like, really good. Really tall stilts, too. And these stilts keep me at a distance, but it's my own doing. It's an easy fix, though. I just have to hop down.

The Bible talks about this place in the temple called the Holy of Holies, or as the English Standard Version calls it, the Most Holy Place. When God gives Moses instructions on how to build the tabernacle, he instructs him that a "'veil shall separate for you the Holy Place from the Most Holy'" (Exodus 26:33), and the presence of God would dwell in the Most Holy Place.

Only the high priest was allowed to enter the Most Holy Place, and not just whenever he wanted. "The priests go regularly into the first section, performing their ritual duties, but into the second only the high priest goes, and he but once a year, and not without taking blood, which he offers for himself and for the unintentional sins of the people" (Hebrews 9:6-7). There are a *lot* of rules about how and when he could enter. Check out Leviticus 16 if you want to read up on that.

But then, fast forward to Jesus. Jesus changed everything, man. And that's not even a cliche. He *actually* changed *everything*. Before, the High Priest had to do all of these rituals to make himself clean, and he would have to perform a very specific sacrifice when he entered the presence of the LORD. Jesus, the very Son of God, died as a sacrifice for you and for me. The final sacrifice. It says in the book of Hebrews that "Christ had offered for all time a single sacrifice for sins" (10:12). And it made us clean so that we could stand before God. And in the very moment that Jesus died, the Bible says that the veil, the one that stood between the average, everyday Israelites and the presence of the Lord, was "torn in two, from top to bottom" (Matthew 27:51).

What does this mean for us? It means that we can now enter the presence of the LORD, without a priest, without a sacrifice. The Most Holy Place is open for us. The veil is no longer keeping us from him. The author of Hebrews continues on to say this:

Therefore, brothers, since we have confidence to enter the holy places by the blood of Jesus, by the new and living way that he opened for us through the curtain, that is, through his flesh, and since we have a great priest over the house of God, let us draw near with a true heart in full assurance of faith (10:19-21).

For much of my life, I have hung out in the outer court. I've been too afraid to enter into the fullness of the presence, ashamed by my unworthiness. And, dare I say, afraid of what I might find, or *not* find. I know that's just the enemy talking. Did you know that in the tabernacle, the place where God's presence dwells, is the Mercy Seat? When we enter into the Most Holy Place, the fullness of his presence, that's exactly what we'll find: mercy.

* * *

I'm trying my best to not hold God at arm's length these days. For me, this looks a lot like being honest with God. About everything. It's kind of ridiculous, because I know that God knows everything, but I used to really sugarcoat things for him. I'd pretend to be fine, pretend to be happy, pretend to be okay with the hard things because I really wanted to trust that God's way was the best way. But, as we all know by now, sometimes God's way is really hard. And to actually come forward and be honest about my real feelings has been a game changer for me.

God can take my hurt and my frustration and my pain and my sadness. I want to be respectful because God is, well, God, and this is a real relationship, but real relationships require honesty. If we don't name our hurt, it's hard to be healed from it. And if we don't get near enough to Jesus to let him see it or touch it, it's even harder.

I've been reading in the book of Mark this month, and I'm awestruck by how often Jesus touches people. Perhaps it's because we're in the middle of a pandemic right now as I write this, and touching others is a big no-no. But that makes it even the more special.

One of my favorite stories is in chapter five—the story of the bleeding woman. She had been bleeding for twelve years and tried everything, and she was finally out of money. But she heard Jesus was in town and knew if she could only touch him, she would be healed. And it was so. She stole a touch when he wasn't looking, but he felt it, even in the middle of a huge crowd. He looked around and asked, "Who touched me!?" And everyone thought that was a pretty ridiculous question, but the woman, trembling, came forward. And Jesus, sweet Jesus, looked at her and called her *daughter* (Mark 5:24-34).

This story happened while Jesus was on his way to heal a little girl. She died while he and the father were on their way, but Jesus continued on. Everyone laughed at him as he announced that the girl was just asleep, but he took her hand anyway, and up she stood (35-43).

In the next chapter, Jesus and his disciples came to Gennesaret, and a crowd instantly formed. Everyone brought their sick friends to Jesus, "that they might touch even the fringe of his garment. And as many as touched it were made well" (56).

The stories go on. Jesus touches the mouths of the mute to make them speak, the ears of the deaf to make them hear, the eyes of the blind to make them see. He touches lepers, even. Jesus is willing to touch even those who are considered *unclean* by the Levitical Law. They just had to get close enough to let him.

In Mark 7, Jesus and his disciples are having a meal and, oops, didn't wash their hands. (Another huge no-no in COVID-19 times.) The Pharisees, as usual, confront Jesus about this disgusting behavior. How dare the disciples eat with defiled hands!? Jesus' response is snarky, "Well did Isaiah prophesy of you hypocrites, as it is written, 'This people honors me with their lips, *but their heart is far from me*'" (7:6, emphasis mine).

Jesus wants to be near to you. He wants to give your wounds the healing touch they need. But how close are you willing to get? He's not the one holding back. Press in. Say yes to drawing near.

* * *

I've never been much of a hiker. Cut me some slack; I come from a place that is quite literally flatter than a pancake. Look it up. Hiking is about that great view at the end, right? You do all this walking and climbing and stumbling and sweating and heavy breathing, all for a magnificent and magical view at the end as your reward. There aren't a whole lot of magnificent and magical views that I have to hike to see back home. Don't get me wrong; there are beautiful sunsets and gorgeous golden fields, but I don't have to get out of my car to see those. I don't have to stumble through the woods. We don't exactly have a whole lot of trees or mountains to block the view in Kansas. In BC, we have to climb an entire mountain to see the horizon (or go to the ocean, I guess). In Kansas, I just have to stand up.

As I started hiking a little more when I moved to British Columbia, I realized hiking wasn't so bad. But, I had a reputation to protect. I was the girl who didn't like hiking. So I kept it on the DL until the pandemic hit, and then people inevitably found out I loved the woods because that's all I did in my free time. It was a little hard to keep it under wraps when that's the only place I could go other than the grocery store once a week.

During my COVID-19 nature walks, I found that I liked to hike by myself more than I did with others. I'm kind of a slow walker. And my lungs aren't used to the altitude, or at least that's what I say. But mostly, it's because I love to look at things. I love stopping and staring up at tall trees. I love stooping down low to look at all the different colors of mushrooms and flowers and little icky bugs. I like to wander around on the side trails and see what I can find. I love to explore.

What I like about exploring is that you have no idea what you're looking for, but you know you're looking for something great! I never set out on an adventure thinking, "Today, I will search and explore until I find the most amazing wild animal in the entire world." Yet, I know that I expect to find something great, because I know the feeling of disappointment when I don't. I've gone on many nature walks that have left me feeling disappointed because they were too short or all the trees were cut down or I was creeped out by a man offering me bottled water out of his backpack (true story).

My walk with Jesus is very much the same. I started out on this journey without knowing what I'm going to find. There is so much to explore, so many paths to wander down, so much to see with him. There's always more, and maybe I'm not sure what's next, but I can be sure something great is in store. Sometimes we stop and look up at all the tall trees, and sometimes I seem to stumble upon some thorns or that nasty stinging nettle; but there's always going to be something beautiful to discover and behold. And while we know that the end view is going to be better than we could ever imagine, something about this exploration part is beautiful and breathtaking in itself, so why not enjoy it?

***

I love that Jesus isn't a salesman. He doesn't try to convince us of anything, really. He's an inviter. He's the kind of guy who is just like, "Yo, come and see for yourself." He's not worried at all about people pulling back the curtain to find out the whole thing is a hoax; he has nothing to worry about. And so his invitation to us is to come and discover. Discover the sweetness.

You could tell somebody all about your favorite dessert using even the most beautiful and decadent adjectives, but that would never beat that person trying it for themselves. Sometimes we're afraid we've hyped something up too much, especially movies or TV shows, only to let someone down because their expectations are so high. But Jesus, *the real Jesus*, he'll never let you down. People are let down by the church all the time, sure. Because the church is a bunch of humans. But Jesus? Nah.

When Jesus called his disciples, he didn't have to do an elevator pitch. He didn't do a PowerPoint presentation on who he was and why they should follow him. His invitation was simple: "'Follow me, and I will make you become fishers of men'" (Mark 1:17). Clear, concise, to the point. And they do; they drop what they're doing and they go with him. They draw close enough to observe it all.

Jesus invites people to come to *him*.

"'Come and you will see,'" he tells two of John the Baptist's disciples (John 1:39).

"'Come and see,'" he invites Nathanael (1:46).

"'If anyone thirsts, let him come to me and drink,'" he declares (7:37).

At one point, Jesus delivers a pretty challenging message, and "many of his disciples turned back and no longer walked with him"

(John 6:66). Jesus turns to the twelve and asks if they want to leave, too. And boy, oh boy, Peter's answer brings tears to my eyes: "'Lord, to whom shall we go? You have the words of eternal life, and we have believed, and have come to know, that you are the Holy One of God'" (68–69).

Jesus doesn't demand that you come to him having it all figured out. He invites you to come along, to walk with him, to watch what he does and how he does it, to live with him, to just believe. And slowly, as you walk with him and watch him, you too will "come to know." You'll see it. You'll get it. You'll know it the way you know the sun will rise every morning.

17

yes to coming to know

The last two weeks of 2019 were the best. I went home to Kansas for Christmas at the tail end of the darkness. I flew out on December 20. The twenty-first was the shortest day of the year—the day of the year we experience the most darkness. It's all uphill after that (until summer solstice of course). I was on the up-and-up, feeling stronger each day. The sun and I both started to shine a little brighter.

Whenever I go back to Kansas, I have a few must-do's:

1. Make a Chick-fil-A drive-thru run with my mom
2. Eat dinner at la Casa de Carrillo
3. Eat brunch and smell candles with Kelli
4. Eat way too many snacks and "watch" a movie (more like talk through a movie) with my besties, Brooke and Emma
5. Snuggle Brooke's baby girl
6. Eat queso from District Taqueria
7. Go to IHOP with my brother
8. Play games with my brother and friends
9. Watch Hallmark movies with my parents
10. Make plans with Catherine for our future house
11. Eat mozzarella sticks with Diane and Carly
12. Go to Target at least once a day

People ask me what I look forward to when I go home, and obviously everything narrows down to the food and the people. Let me tell you guys, people who say that Canada and the USA aren't that different are wrong. I get pretty heated when people "joke" about culture shock, as if I didn't experience it. Oh, I had culture shock alright. But it happened a little differently than in most other countries I've been in. The longer I've stayed, the more differences I've noticed. And all of the big differences that were hard for me to get over were either about, you guessed it, food or people.

I grew up in the Midwest eating a lot of bread, potatoes, noodles, fried food, and canned vegetables. Meat was always there, but I didn't really like it as a kid. Many people here in BC prefer a greener and leafier diet. My major complaints about the food is the lack of sketchy Chinese buffets, the fact that I cannot find queso blanco or fried mozzarella sticks anywhere, and where I am supposed to get my cheap fast Italian food? And Mexican food!? And don't even get me started on my donut cravings. I'm craving a big fluffy glazed donut from *LaMar's* right this minute.

The food problems I learned to manage fairly quickly. I'm probably a healthier individual for it. But learning to navigate the way relationships work here was different. It took me a long time to put my finger on why I was struggling so much to make friends here. I'm good at making friends—at least, I thought I was. Like, if that was something people put on resumes, I would. Right at the top. But it was not as easy as I anticipated. People are busy up here! People plan ahead here! But here's the biggest thing I finally figured out: many people in my circles here are one-on-one kind of people, rather than group kind of people. And even though it drove me nuts at first (I love a good group hang out, a loud party, and a bunch of friends and strangers gathered around the table), I've learned to see so much beauty in it.

Most of my friend hangs these days look like two or three of us chatting over coffee. And though I have fewer friends than I did back in Kansas, I would venture to say that some of my friends here know me on a deeper level than some of the friends I have had for years back home.

But I have to say, going home is always a breath of fresh air. There's just something about being known. About familiarity. About not needing a map to go somewhere, even if you've never been there before. About getting to eat the food you grew up with and going to stores and knowing exactly what is in every aisle. About going to church and receiving a dozen hugs from people you haven't seen in months. Oh, my heart feels full even just thinking about it.

A trip home was exactly what my heart needed. The fall had seemed to last an eternity, and to end a very hard year with people I don't have to explain myself to, my people, felt like the best Christmas gift ever.

* * *

I love reading the story of Elizabeth and Zechariah in Luke 1 each Christmas season. It's such a *human* story. Zechariah was a priest, and his wife's name was Elizabeth. The Bible says that "they were both righteous before God" (1:6). Elizabeth couldn't have kids, and they're pretty old by the time we get to this story.

Zechariah was chosen to enter the temple to burn incense. This was a pretty big deal, as we discussed in the last chapter. And what makes Zechariah's experience even more magnificent is that while he was in there, an angel appeared to him with a message from God! And what makes *that* even more significant is that this is believed to be the silence-breaking moment of God's "400 years of silence." Meaning, Zechariah may well have been the first person to hear God speak in at least 400 years.

The angel tells Zechariah something wild. Something he never saw coming: Elizabeth, his "advanced-in-years" wife, was going to get pregnant with a baby boy. And that baby boy, who was to be named John, was going to change the world. And how does Zechariah respond?

Disbelief.

Here's another instance where we, as the readers with more information than Zechariah had at the time, scoff. Come on, Zechariah. How could you not believe an angel!? But let's be real; I'd have a hard time believing it myself if I was in his sandals. I mean, Elizabeth is *old*.

The angel isn't too pleased with Zechariah's response, though. So in turn, Zechariah is muted. Can't speak a single word.

Fast-forward to the birth of the baby: Everyone thought the boy should be given a family name, but Zechariah remembered the angel's instruction. He still couldn't speak, so he pulls out some kind of tablet and writes, "His name is John" (1:63). Everyone thought it was kind of weird, choosing a name that doesn't run in the family. But in that moment, Zechariah's tongue is loosed and he is able to speak again.

I relate to this story not because of the circumstance (I am *not* an elderly woman giving birth, nor an elderly priest), but because of what Zechariah perhaps learned in this experience. After coming out of a season when I struggled with fear and doubt, I saw something that Christmas that I had never put together: *Disbelief silences us. Obedience sets us free.*

Could I believe the promises that God had given me? That good things were to come? That new things were to come? That I was on my way to blooming and growing and flourishing? That spring was on its way? Could I believe that the new year had something good in store for me? That all of this suffering was truly unto something? I did not want the enemy to hold my tongue any longer. I did not want to be silenced any longer.

* * *

I looked forward to the new year. I love any excuse to spend time reflecting and journaling and thinking of what could be. I do it for the new year, my birthday (which is only about six weeks later), and the first of July every year. Minimum. I don't set a ton of measurable goals, but I like to look back at what I've learned and ask God for a word and what I need to grow in. Some of my goals for 2020 included cultivating more discipline in my life, getting to know the character of Jesus better, writing this book (!!!), running more, and scrolling less. My word for the year was one you've heard before: yes.

My first journal entry of 2020 starts out like this: "2020. What a big-sounding year. The world has big expectations, 2020. You best not let us all down."

Let's all pause for at least two minutes to laugh until we cry at the irony of this statement. Wow, we had no idea what 2020 had in store for all of us, did we?

I came back to BC a few days into the New Year, January 3 or 4 I think. I was a little nervous to come back, to be honest. I had a few hard nights in Wichita, but they were becoming less and less frequent. What if I started to experience fear, anxiety, or doubt again? I remembered the story of Zechariah. I didn't want disbelief to rule my story. I held onto the promises of something new. Something good was coming. Last year, I had to choose to believe. I wanted this year to be the year I came to *know*.

As I mentioned earlier, one of my "goals" for the new year was to get to know the character of Jesus better. I wanted to know, really know, who Jesus was. To observe him, to learn from him, to fall in love with him. And so, I dedicated this entire year to reading the Gospels: Matthew, Mark, Luke, and John. The original plan was to read them each three times (one whole Gospel each month of the year). That hasn't exactly happened.

For some reason I started in the Gospel of John. It took me three months to read. Not because I forgot to read or because I have the reading comprehension of a first grader, mind you, but because it is so good. So good. So. Good. I could barely read five verses without pausing to make notes in my journal about what Jesus was doing. I started making lists and lists of things I saw about Jesus, finishing the sentence, "Jesus is…"

One morning, I think the morning I read John 6 actually, I was literally so in awe and excited about what I had learned that I caught myself mindlessly repeating the phrase, "Jesus is dope! Jesus is dope!" as I washed my breakfast dishes. It made me laugh, but it also caused my soul to worship—seeing how far he had already brought me into the light.

* * *

I learned a lot about Jesus just from the Gospel of John. There's something about slowly combing the text, looking for descriptions of who he is as a person that changes your perspective.

Jesus really, really loved people. As I read, I saw how he is close to people. How he sees people. How he doesn't ignore people. How he speaks to them and really meets their needs. I saw how he has feelings about people: he has compassion for them. He is grieved by their deaths. He is grieved by their hard hearts.

When you read the Bible to get to know him, you start to look at Jesus a whole lot more than you look at yourself. I cannot tell you how much this has helped and healed me after my season of darkness, fear, and—if I'm honest—self-obsession.

The year isn't over yet; it's still 2020 as I write today. I'm in the middle of the book of Mark right now. Matthew is next. I'm still not sure why I'm doing them backwards, really. But what I am sure of is this: I will never know everything about Jesus, but I'm thankful for what I do know, and about all the things about him I will come to know in the years ahead. It's exciting to me that there is always more to learn, more to see, more to experience; and, when it comes to the person of Jesus, it will always be good.

As I write today I'm sitting on our back balcony. The twinkly string of lights overhead are lit, creating a warm glow on my yellow-painted toenails. A cool breeze is blowing, even though it's mid-July. Perks of living in Canada. With a blanket spread out on the floor, I'm leaning against a pillow and the sliding door. I'm reminded of a moment with Jesus back in December.

I was seated, just as I am now, but upstairs in my room against the wall. Eyes closed, asking Jesus what he wanted me to hear that day. And I visualized Jesus, sweet Jesus, sitting there next to me. Close. Hip to hip. His head was on my shoulder. And together we sat quiet, like close friends just appreciating the presence of one another. I feel him here now. And I pray you feel him, too.

18

yes to peace

I left for Thailand with a knot in my stomach. I was traveling alone, with a long flight ahead of me, but that wasn't why I was nervous. I looked in the mirror one hour before my roommate drove me to the airport that night and asked God if I was really supposed to go. This new and novel Coronavirus was spreading across China like wildfire, and while there were only about twenty-five cases in Thailand, I felt a little anxious.

My flight was fine, but the layover was a little confusing. Some people had to fill out special paperwork, some didn't. Hallways were blocked off and long lines marked off for people to speak with airport workers sitting at tables. There were specific lineups for people to get screened, but I didn't have to because I was getting on a connecting flight.

The purpose of my trip was to meet up with a team of our students serving there, in the same churches I had served only two years earlier. I was excited to see the team of four girls, the missionaries, and my Thai friends. A missionary friend and I were taking the girls up north in a few days to Chiang Mai to facilitate a retreat for them.

The trip started out fairly well, but I could tell some people were nervous around me since I had been traveling. When the day arrived to take the overnight bus the thirteen hours up north, anxiety had started to rise in many of our friends. One of the women from the church had received word that if the girls were to travel to Chiang Mai as planned, they'd have to be quarantined for fourteen days upon their return. This sounded absolutely absurd to me. Looking back and remembering this moment, I can't believe how normal the thought of quarantining has become.

We made the call last minute to not travel. Literally fifteen minutes before we were due to leave for the bus station. The purpose of the retreat was to refuel the team to serve well for the next three months. If they couldn't leave their rooms for two weeks, this seemed to defeat the purpose! We booked a hotel on the beach an hour away and reworked the retreat. I started to stress out as the anxiety around me was escalating. Would I be able to make it out of Thailand?

Then the unthinkable happened. I woke up one morning with a fever and achy body. My anxiety skyrocketed. I was supposed to fly home in a few days, and I already had to rebook my flight once! The retreat ended the next morning, and I still had a low-grade fever. I told my host when I returned to her house, and we prayed about what to do.

The next day was possibly one of the strangest days of my life and will forever be etched in my memory. My host took me to the hospital to do our due diligence. My fever was incredibly low. So low that it didn't even register when they screened me at the hospital. But we explained why we were there, and it set the nurses off in a tizzy. We waited for about an hour outside the hospital, answering questions, talking to various people about when I was traveling, etc. People were panicking. I looked around with confusion, because honestly, I wasn't even showing any symptoms anymore.

Finally, one of the employees said my room was ready. (Keep in mind, all of this was in Thai, and my Thai is limited to food and directions and "Hi-I-teach-free-English-at-the-Hope-Center-every-Thursday-night." My host was translating for me.) The man led us around to the back of the hospital, and we went in the back entrance to a rickety elevator. He pressed the button for the ninth floor.

The doors opened, and I was greeted by two nurses in white hazmat suits. They sternly scolded the man for letting my host come up with me and sent them both back downstairs. I started to panic. None of the nurses spoke English. They led me into a nearly empty room where eight beds were evenly spread out. A nurse patted one bed, and I understood the word "sleep." I told her in Thai that I did not understand. The other nurse pulled out her phone and searched for a translation. She held it out for me to read: "You sleep here twelve hours."

Twelve hours!? My jaw dropped. I looked around the room wildly. I tried to explain that my friend just went downstairs; could they call her please? After a few minutes, they handed me the phone. My friend confirmed that, yes, I was to stay there twelve hours, and she wasn't allowed to come back upstairs. I started to cry, and the nurses were alarmed. I assured them it was fine, but I was truly scared.

I didn't have any data to contact my parents or my friends or anyone to let them know what was going on or to ask them to pray. I hadn't eaten lunch yet, and it was already one o'clock. My phone was only at 53%, and that definitely wouldn't last me twelve hours of game playing or music listening. It sounds dramatic, perhaps, but I'd be lying if I said I didn't lie there and cry for about an hour. It wasn't a sob or a weep, but just gentle tears steadily trickling down my warm cheeks onto the plastic mattress.

Around hour two, I pulled out my journal, which conveniently was one of the only things in my backpack. By hour three and a half, the nurse brought me a plastic bag containing my favorite meal from one of my favorite restaurants in town and a phone card so I could keep people updated. By hour four, the nurse came in and said in broken English, "Return home, 10 minutes."

I sat up and stared at her, confused. Was I really being released in ten minutes? I should have eight more hours to go! But sure enough, in about twenty minutes, they came in and took me back down the elevator to where my friend was waiting for me. I was fine, and it was over.

***

When I finally made it back to Canada, our world was already on its way to never being the same again. Little did I know that my birthday party, just a few days before I left for my trip, would be the last night for a long time I'd be surrounded by friends, laughing till our faces hurt.

I was in self-isolation upon my arrival home, and the day it ended was the day our office closed. Coronavirus had arrived in BC. More time at home, yay. I struggled with health nearly the entire month of March: bronchitis led to strep throat which led to a very unsightly skin infection on my face. My trip back to Kansas was canceled in April. People were hoarding toilet paper, and hand sanitizer was nowhere to be found. There were new rules every day about how many people we could spend time with and where we could go. Stores and restaurants and parks were closing. I didn't see some of my friends for months. Church and work were both online.

Early on, I just wanted to fall asleep. I wanted to ignore everything going on, plug my ears to the horror stories, and pretend it wasn't happening. I could blissfully live in my house for a few weeks and just pretend it was a little retreat, easy. I was discouraged and frustrated, and a little anxious too.

Then, one night, as I lay on the couch and contemplated deleting all my online connections to the outside world, I had a revelation. Picture an ocean in a storm, the waves huge and scary. In the middle of the waves sits one still boat with a large anchor. I realized that I am not called to hide away, or go fall asleep somewhere on the shore, but I'm called to be the calm, the steady, and the still in the middle of the chaos. I have an anchor in Jesus, and because of this, I am able to be a steady, safe, peaceful place where others can seek harbor.

* * *

I've always loved Philippians 4. I come back to this chapter on a regular basis, as it's brought much encouragement to my heart over the years. And yet, in the middle of the chaos of all that is and was 2020, I realized that I never really *believed* it.

"Do not be anxious about anything, but in everything by prayer and supplication with thanksgiving let your requests be made known to God. And the peace of God, which surpasses all understanding, will guard your hearts and your minds in Christ Jesus" (Philippians 4:6-7).

Did you catch that first phrase? No? Here it is again: "Do not be anxious about anything."

Anything.

If Paul is charging us to not be anxious about anything, not a single thing, that must mean that it's possible. It's possible to not be anxious about moving. About a job change. About a worldwide pandemic. About the elections. About what the future holds. About finances. About your relationship. Anything.

I had every reason to be anxious during the spring of 2020. We all did. We all still do. But we don't have to. We are told not to.

In John 14, Jesus said, "Peace I leave with you, my peace I give to you. Not as the world gives do I give to you. Let not your hearts be troubled, neither let them be afraid" (14:27).

He knew we had reason to be afraid, to be nervous, to be anxious. That's why Jesus promised us he'd give us peace! Peace that "surpasses all understanding," according to the Philippians passage.

But sweet Jesus said he wouldn't give as the world gives. When the world gives, it gives expecting something in return. It's a give-and-take kind of system. The world gives in a competitive fashion, always trying to one-up someone else. The world often gives out of pure duty or obligation, not from a generous heart. The world gives with strings attached, in measured quantities, and as sparingly as possible. But Jesus...Jesus gives freely. He gives, expecting nothing in return. He gives in abundance, offering more than we could ever need. He gives because he loves.

So if this is how Jesus gives us peace—freely, in abundance, expecting nothing in return—why do so many of us fail to experience peace?

Well, remember when I talked about how surprised I was when I realized how much I like to be in control? Yeah. Lack of peace for me comes down to my desire to be in control. Maybe it does for you, too.

Most of my anxiety comes from worrying about the future, making plans, or trying to control what is going to happen. And that, my friend, is refusing peace because it's refusing to trust that God is in control.

His peace surpasses understanding. Trust, especially when we don't understand, leads us to peace.

When there is a circumstance I can't control, I fall in one of two camps of extremists: I either freak out and encounter serious anxiety, or, I fall asleep to all problems of the world. Ignorance is bliss...am I right? Yet, there is a place of peace in between these two camps: the place where we can recognize the problem or situation at hand and still remain at peace despite those circumstances.

As followers of Christ, we are invited to be the still boat on the raging waves. I want to be a safe place for my friends to gather in the midst of panic. Jesus actually *slept* on the boat in the storm, he was so at peace! We too can join sleeping Jesus and rest in his presence.

* * *

I was at small groups about a year ago, and for an icebreaker question we were asked to use one word to describe our week. Person after person described their week as "busy" or "exhausting" or "long" or "rough," and my heart grew heavy as they shrugged their shoulders as if to say, "Such is life. This is the way it's supposed to be."

My heart yearns for more. For more than busy schedules and long working hours and exhausting social engagements. My heart longs for rest. For peace. For abundance. We're supposedly the generation of self-care, but we seem to be doing a pretty bad job of caring for our souls.

Jesus talks about abundant living in John 10:10 when he says, "The thief comes only to steal and kill and destroy. I came that they may have life and have it abundantly." What does it look like to live abundantly in a season of panic? Of chaos? Of working long hours only to come home to a crying newborn baby? Of trying to make ends meet? Of a worldwide pandemic?

Jesus isn't behind the busyness our world craves, I don't think. It's not him stealing precious hours of your sleep, destroying your relationships, or killing your joy. That's the thief (a.k.a. Satan). Jesus wants you to live abundantly! Vibrantly! Joyfully! Jesus offers us peace; he offers us rest! What is it about busy-ness that our world values so much? I don't want to feel ashamed anymore for *not* having weekend plans and being excited about it. I don't want to feel guilty for saying "awesome" when people ask me how I'm doing. I don't want to feel bad that I'm not burnt out when we have those real-talk circles at work.

I want to give my all for Jesus, but I don't think that looks like what we think it looks like. I think it looks like being at peace. Like being awed at the sunrise every single morning. Like having thriving relationships with your family and friends and coworkers and neighbors. Like being obedient, even when it doesn't quite make sense. It probably looks a little messy and a little weird to the rest of the world, but I think it looks pretty colorful and vibrant and beautiful. Maybe like an abstract painting that nobody quite understands but the artist himself.

You may be tired today, and your world may be crashing down, but I want to remind you of something: The Father will heal. He will mend. He will bring clarity, and he will speak. He will make good, like he always does. He won't push before you're ready, or look at you with a furrowed brow. As you sit in the dust with broken pieces all around you, he will humbly come, crouch down, and sit with an arm around your shoulder. Just waiting, present, ready to speak whenever you're ready to listen, and ready to listen whenever you're ready to speak.

19

yes to the hard work

I pulled into the parking lot at Mill Lake one afternoon when I noticed them. I squinted a little bit and tilted my head, like a confused pup. I got out of my car and looked around to see if I missed something. But no, nothing out of the ordinary. There they sat: two elderly women, happy as can be, chatting away in lawn chairs in the middle of a parking lot swarming with cars and people.

Mill Lake may not be the best park in Abbotsford, but you could do a lot worse. You can enjoy a lot of green space, a lake (obviously), lots of benches and covered picnic areas, playgrounds, etc. And these two women chose to come all the way to the park, just to sit in the parking lot. It perplexed me then, and it perplexes me now. They could have seen and done so much more! Or chosen one of so many more half decent places to sit.

A few months later, I was on vacation with my roommate. We heard about a lookout point where you could drive up to watch the sunset. With only minutes to spare, we flew up the mountain and scrambled out of the car. There, just about twenty feet from the parking lot, people were congregated at the railing to take pictures. It was breathtaking. The sky was a gorgeous backdrop behind city lights below. I pulled out my camera. My roommate pointed up and to the right, though.

"Let's go up there!" She headed towards a path. We weren't dressed for a hike, but luckily it wasn't very far. We rushed up, passing some who were already on their way down. We reached the peak only minutes later, and wow. Wow. A 360-degree view of mountains, ocean, and city in front of a canvas of pinks and oranges and purples. What a difference that extra little hike up made. It was so breathtaking, so awe-inspiring, that we went back the next night for more.

* * *

I was a straight-A student in high school, and I definitely was not a procrastinator. I liked school for the most part, and I liked working on projects. My friends were mostly smart, and thirteen of us graduated with Valedictorian status from my class.

Likewise, I put a lot of effort into my job (most of the time). I want my work to be done with excellence. I never considered myself a procrastinator or one to do just enough to get by. I've always been seen as responsible and thorough. And yet, a few years ago, I started noticing all these things on the side…all the unfinished projects piling up on my desk at home. Planners that were left at least half blank. Novels with bookmarks still in the middle. Running shoes used only a handful of times. YouTube videos paused with a few minutes left; tabs open to read later; you get it.

How had I never noticed this before? I was, in fact, a quitter! Me! Becky Spahr! When there was nobody to please but myself, no one else depending on me, I would just give up when I got bored. In school, I needed to please my teachers and my parents. At work, I need to please my boss and my co-workers. The work of others depends on me completing mine. The participants in our programs depend on me to do my job well. But when it's just for me? Forget it. I'm out as soon as the road gets a little bumpy.

I see it in the way that I can't seem to stick to an exercise routine. I see it in my eating habits. The fact that this book is in your hands right now is something I can hardly believe; I didn't quit. I finished the book. I saw something all the way through. Something that nobody was waiting on, something that was a secret for a long time. As much as I wrote this for you, friend, I finished it for me.

Writing this book has been a season of learning to say yes to the hard work. Of learning *discipline*. I don't think it's an accident that I'm writing a book, getting into running, and trying to work from home all at the same time. These are three things that have required much intentionality and discipline on my part. And trust me when I say that I almost gave up on all three. I took a month-long break from writing. I took a longer break from running. And some days, if I'm completely honest, I just stared at my computer and ended up grocery shopping when I was supposed to be working.

I don't like hard things. I don't like challenging myself. You know me enough by now: I love comfort. I like *good enough*. I live in a world of good enough. And I think that I've been okay with settling for less in a lot of areas of life. I've been okay with sitting in the parking lot instead of right on the lake. But right now, God has been teaching me not to settle for less than the best. Less than *his* best, that is.

* * *

I believe that God has abundant life in store for each one of us, like I mentioned in the last chapter. God's definition for abundant life may not be what we think of in human terms (money, power, excess), but how many times have those things actually fulfilled you? Getting a raise at work gives off a temporary high, but it doesn't last long. Power is pretty cool I suppose, until things go awry. And having an excess of stuff doesn't mean you don't want *more*.

Jesus offers an abundance of other things. An abundance of hope. Of joy. Of peace. Of community. Of purpose. These are what we should pursue. These are what we should put in the work to attain.

Let's go back to the Old Testament and talk about the Israelites one more time. God used Moses to rescue them from slavery and oppression in Egypt, right? So you would think they'd be a grateful group of people, right? The text says otherwise.

Before the people even crossed the Red Sea, they were complaining and grumbling! "'Is it because there are no graves in Egypt that you have taken us away to die in the wilderness? What have you done to us in bringing us out of Egypt?'" (Exodus 14:11)

Then they ride the high of seeing God's miraculous power for a while, but soon they're right back at it in Exodus 17:3 when they ask, "'Why did you bring us up out of Egypt, to kill us and our children and our livestock with thirst?'"

God provides magical food from the sky called manna for them to eat, but then they get tired of it after a bit. "'We remember the fish we ate in Egypt that cost nothing, the cucumbers, the melons, the leeks, the onions, and the garlic'" (Numbers 11:5).

And then, they finally see this Promised Land, Canaan, with their own eyes but are too scared to take the land, so, naturally, why not go back to Egypt? "'Why is the LORD bringing us into this land, to fall by the sword? Our wives and our little ones will become a prey. Would it not be better for us to go back to Egypt?...Let us choose a leader and go back to Egypt!'" (Numbers 14:3-4)

The pattern we see throughout the entire journey to the Promised Land (God's promise for abundant life) is that when the situation gets a little tough, when the Israelites need to put in a little bit of elbow grease, when things aren't going their way, they want to go back to Egypt. They want to go back to the way things were, to the *good enough* life. To the familiar and comfortable. Why go through all of this for something that is supposedly "great" if what we had before was good enough?

It pains me to admit it, but I know that I'd be a complaining Israelite. I know I'd want to go back. I know I'd romanticize the past. I'd be the one dreaming of the cucumbers and the melons and the leeks (okay, how funny is that verse!?). But I don't want to be known for that.

* * *

Last week I took a day to spend with Jesus. At my job we get one "prayer day" a month. Eight hours is a long time to pray, and it sounds scary and kind of boring if I'm honest, so I usually refer to them as "Jesus days" instead. I spend time in the presence of the Lord. I do pray, and I also read, and I listen, and I enjoy.

So, on Friday, I drove into Vancouver to do something I've been wanting to do for a few months: visit the conservatory at Queen Elizabeth Park. I love plants and flowers. I know next to nothing about them, but, as you've read, the LORD just keeps speaking to me about gardens and greenhouses and blooming.

The conservatory didn't open until 11:00 am, but I went early to enjoy some time at the park first. I found a bench between the parking lot and the conservatory and took a seat with my journal, but after about fifteen minutes, I decided I should do a little exploring. I had read online that there were a few gardens at the park, so I set out to find them.

It's hard to explain what I felt the moment I found myself surrounded by bushes and trees and flowers galore. Tears sprang to my eyes a handful of times as I wound around and around on the paths, gasping as I rounded each curve. Oranges and purples and pinks exploded from the ground. Patterns of succulents formed on one side of the path, and ferns and other green, leafy plants hugged the other. My heart felt like it might explode.

I thought about how I almost missed this to just sit on a bench for an hour. Because that was good enough.

I felt the LORD impress on my heart that *this* is what everything was unto. I hadn't been pruned and transplanted and raked over to be a run-of-the-mill flower bed in someone's backyard. If we join God in the hard work, if we lean into it, our lives will be more than just *good enough*.

Even though much of the physical world seems to be falling apart around me, I've seen many of God's promises over my life come to fruition this year. I attended a conference last spring where a team of prayer warriors and intercessors wrote notes and hung them on the wall. We were invited to read them and take one if we felt like it resonated with us. One practically jumped off the wall at me that read, "The year of FLOWERING: what was planted last year is now producing Big Blooms."

That word didn't happen for me last year, as much as I wanted it to. Obviously, I kind of fell apart last year. I felt like my flowers just fell off and died last year. But this year, today, this word is for me. This year, somehow, by the grace of God, I'm blooming. I'm flowering. I'm flourishing. In the middle of illness and deaths and suicides and loneliness and panic happening around me, God has given me the strength and the joy to thrive.

* * *

So here's what I'm learning about discipline: self-discipline doesn't just show up. You can wait around forever waiting to feel motivated, but it will likely never show up on your doorstep holding your running shoes in one hand and your computer keyboard in the other. If you want to lose weight, you have to start running. And you have to *keep* running. If you want a book on your shelf with your name on it, you have to start writing. And *keep* writing. Even when it's hard. Even when you want to quit. If you want to keep your job, you have to work. Even if you don't really *feel* like it. Because remember what we learned in chapter one? Feelings don't dictate truth.

Saying yes to Jesus takes discipline. I didn't even realize that he was building endurance in me. (But that's what discipline does, doesn't it?) He's asked me to do progressively harder things over the years, one step, one yes, at a time. And it gets easier, it really does, because this is what I have been training for. Jesus doesn't expect you to be able to say the hardest yes of your entire life the morning after you gave your life to him. He's kinder than that. He starts small and builds up. Unfortunately, some of us get stuck early on.

The book of Matthew contains a parable about a master and three servants. The master gives each of his servants a different amount of money and then goes on a journey. When he comes back, the servants report to him what they've done with the money. The first doubled what he had, as did the second. But the third, who was given the least amount of money, was so afraid of losing what his master had given him that he buried it in the ground. The master was so furious that he called him a "wicked and slothful servant" and gave his money to the first servant (Matthew 25:14–20, paraphrased).

I don't know about you, but I don't ever want my Master, Jesus, to look at me and call me a "wicked and slothful servant." I don't want to waste what gifts he's given me, whether it's finances or abilities or time. I don't want to be too lazy to put in the work. I believe that God made us with our specific gifts and abilities and assets to yield fruit for his kingdom! I have certain abilities that allow me to reach certain people, and you have different abilities that allow you to reach different people. May we not shrink back and hide out of fear, and may we not grow lazy.

My prayer is that God would activate our generation to use the gifts he's given us to reach people in new ways. Creativity and ingenuity abound in our world today! May we use it for his glory and not for ourselves or our status or our fame. I had a thought the other day at breakfast that may or may not be theologically sound, but here goes: Do you think that if every single person *actually* stepped into their God-given identity—if we all actually did our part and stepped into the hard things—the whole world would be saved? I don't know, but I like to think so. If the Body truly functioned like a Body, if we all walked in complete obedience, if we all knew the authority we have in Jesus' name, I think the world would look completely different. I really want to do my part. And I pray that you do, too.

20

yes to abiding

It all started with a garden and a Holy Gardener. And it all restarted with a Gardener, too. The women visited Jesus' tomb early on the third day. Mary Magdalene was there, and she discovered the tomb to be empty. Weeping, she saw a man standing near the tomb. *The gardener*, she thought. They spoke a bit, until he said the word that opened her eyes to the reality of a resurrected Jesus standing in front of her: "Mary" (John 20:16). Her name was all it took.

There's something about someone using your name that can make you feel known and loved in an instant. We get excited when someone important knows our name. We get butterflies when our high school crush says our name in a sentence. To think that Jesus knows and *uses* my name fills me with awe and wonder. The Creator, the Gardener, the Almighty God...knows *my* name?

Do you really think it was an accident that Mary mistook Jesus for a gardener in this moment? I can't say that I do. Just as the beginning of humankind started with man walking with God in the garden, the beginning of new resurrection life does as well.

As much as I believe that Jesus wants us to be obedient and do hard things and live *for* him, I believe that Jesus, maybe even more than those things, wants us to be *with* him. To walk *with* him. To do life *with* him.

When Jesus narrowed down his following to the twelve disciples, he didn't just give them an assignment and send them on their way. He called them to himself, to relationship. To be with him. Mark's telling of the story says, "And he [Jesus] went up on the mountain and called to him those whom he desired, and they came to him. And he appointed twelve (whom he also named apostles) *so that they might be with him* and *he might send them out to preach* and *have authority to cast out demons*" (3:13-15, emphasis mine).

I see three things that Jesus wanted for these twelve men, and the first thing on the list was for them to be with him. Oh, how my heart just swoons when I read things like this. Jesus is a people person. Jesus is speaking my language here. One of the things that exhausts me most is when I ask someone to hang out with me, and their immediate response is, "What do you want to do?" I don't want to *do anything*; I just want to *be with you*! My primary love language is quality time, and I have to wonder if Jesus' is, too.

Second, Jesus appoints the apostles to preach. While the act of simply being with him comes first, a mission still needs to be carried out: sharing, preaching, and teaching the good news. This should flow out of a place of being with Jesus. Our being with him informs what and how we preach. To skip out on experiencing Jesus for ourselves would make our message less effective.

And thirdly, Jesus gives his disciples the authority to cast out demons. To overcome darkness with light. To usher in the freedom that comes with knowing and living life with Jesus. As believers and followers of Christ, we have been given authority. We are no longer enslaved to the powers and principalities of darkness. Ephesians 6 says that we can "stand against the schemes of the devil" (6:11), and that our fight is "against the rulers, against the authorities, against the cosmic powers of this present darkness, against the spiritual forces of evil in the heavenly places" (6:12). Luke 9:10 says that Jesus gives us authority "over all the power of the enemy."

What is important to remember is that the calling of a disciple (not just the Twelve, but *all of us* who follow Jesus) is threefold. Some of us get fixated on the first part, being with Jesus, and we forget to carry out the mission. Another group of us are passionate teachers and preachers, and yet we actually forego spending time with the one who called us. And some of us do pretty well at the first two, and yet we are too afraid to actually use the authority Christ has given us, while others are so caught up in healing and freedom that, again, we forget to be with Jesus and preach his message.

All three are good things; otherwise, Jesus wouldn't have appointed his apostles to do all three. And one or two of these will come more naturally to us than others. But that doesn't excuse us from growing in each area.

* * *

I don't know where you are in your journey with Jesus, but I want to invite you to say yes to his invitation to be with him: to abide. "Abide" is a word that I haven't heard much outside of the church, and even though many of us use it, I'm unsure that we actually know what it means.

John 15 is the famous "abide" passage. In the ESV translation, I see this word used ten times! Let's start with verse 4:

> Abide in me, and I in you. As the branch cannot bear fruit by itself, unless it abides in the vine, neither can you, unless you abide in me. I am the vine; you are the branches. Whoever abides in me and I in him, he it is that

bears much fruit, for apart from me you can do nothing. If anyone does not abide in me he is thrown away like a branch and withers; and the branches are gathered, thrown into the fire, and burned. If you abide in me, and my words abide in you, ask whatever you wish, and it will be done for you. By this my Father is glorified, that you bear much fruit and so prove to be my disciples. As the Father has loved me, so have I loved you. Abide in my love. If you keep my commandments, you will abide in my love, just as I have kept my Father's commandments and abide in his love. These things I have spoken to you, that my joy may be in you, and that your joy may be full (15:4–11).

That's a lot of abiding. But, what does that mean? The New Living Translation uses the word "remain"; the Passion translation uses the phrase "remain in life-union"; and the Message translation uses words like "live" and "make your home." There's a sense of togetherness. Connection. Intimacy.

In this particular passage, Jesus calls himself the true vine (15:1), and we are the branches. We, as branches, are to stay connected to the vine. If you break a branch or a stick or a twig off a tree, you can't do much with it other than use it for firewood. Staying connected to Jesus, being with him, living with him, is what brings us life.

The other night at Bible study, a group of girls and I were discussing what it actually looks like to "believe" in Jesus. And as we chatted, I found my heart longing to just love Jesus more. To just be with him more.

We talked about how believing looks more like trust than it does intellectual agreement. To believe in Jesus means to entrust him with our hearts and our lives. Even the demons *know* that Jesus is real (James 2:19), but they definitely have not handed over their hearts.

Our group leader encouraged us to think about it in the context of engagement, or betrothal. It's a commitment. A relationship. A choice. A coming together. A joining. Love is involved, but not based on only temporary feelings or emotions. You make choices in a way that honors the other person. You trust that person with your heart.

I don't want to fall into the legalism of obeying Jesus without actually trusting him. I want to actually believe that he is the best thing. That he is the greatest thing that life could ever, ever offer me. I actually want to be in love with him. I actually want to mean it when I say that he is better than clothes or boys or Kansas or friends. And the only way I will get to that place is if I take the time to abide.

Jesus calls himself the "true vine." This tells me that there are other vines out there. And when I find myself down in the dumps or moody or irritated, I've started asking myself, "In which vine am I abiding?" And often, it isn't the true vine. Sometimes I abide in Netflix. I just watch and watch and watch. And I feel lazy and sad. Other times, I abide in my own thoughts. I can get lost in my mind, turning in circles of "what ifs." And I feel anxious and fearful. But abiding in Jesus? Jesus says abiding in him brings good fruit. It brings love. It brings him glory. It brings joy. And that makes me feel pretty stinking good.

* * *

This book is all about yeses, and sweet friend, I don't want to make any assumptions about you. I push people to say yes, I do. I really, really want to see people living and walking in obedience to Jesus Christ. But maybe you're reading this book, and it's all very hard to comprehend because you haven't even said the first "yes" yet.

If that's you, I first want to say thank you for reading this far. And second, I want to hold your face in my hands (very close, and maybe a little uncomfortably), look you right in your bright and beautiful eyes, and tell you that Jesus wants to be with you.

He doesn't need you to say all these other yeses first. He doesn't need you to have anything figured out. He doesn't need you to clean up your act or remove your piercings or read the entire Bible first. That's the whole reason Jesus came to earth. He stepped down into this mess to be with us, to make a way for us to be together for eternity. He didn't wait until we all made this a better place. He didn't have the Father flood the earth again and start over again. He came down to the earth, just as it was—to us, just as we were—to dwell among the people he loves.

And so, before you say no to this whole Jesus-life thing, try a tiny yes. Give the first yes a go. Say yes to being with him. To just trying it. Say yes to allowing him to prove you all wrong. Say yes to the possibility that he could actually be real and alive and at work. What could you possibly have to lose?

21

yes to what's next

I don't know what's next for me, and I definitely don't know what's next for you. I don't really make a lot of plans anymore, if I'm honest. I like to dream, sure. But I've learned that coming up with a five- or ten-year plan takes a lot of time and energy and brain space, and it doesn't usually end up the way I expect it to anyway.

I wrote this entire book in Canada. By the time it's in your hands, though, I probably won't even live in Canada anymore. It's strange to think that I'll be doing something completely different by this time next year, and I have no idea what that something is. Or where. When people ask me what my future plans are, I usually respond with, "Who's really to say?"

God says, that's who. And I'm waiting on him to clue me in. Oh, I have some ideas, I guess. But nothing I'm sure about yet. I'm encouraged that, even though I don't really know, I'm not anxious. This, for me, is a sign of growth. A few months ago, I was praying about my future and felt an overwhelming sense of peace. "Aha!" I wrote in my journal, "*This* must be what trust feels like."

I think I'm slowly learning how to, in the words of Hannah Brencher, be where my feet are. I'm learning to stand on one stepping stone at a time, instead of straddling two or three. I'm looking at the next exit on the highway, instead of the one a few miles ahead. I know that whatever Jesus brings my way next, I will say yes to. So why worry about it now?

Of course I need to put in the work on my end (apply for jobs, pray for wisdom, seek the counsel of others), but "which of you by being anxious can add a single hour to his span of life?" (Matthew 6:27). I have found that trusting God, really trusting him, with my life and my heart is a game changer. When our yeses are unconditional, we are better versions of ourselves. I've already chosen to say yes, and so I sleep better. I have more fun. I love others better. I am less distracted. I am relaxed.

It feels easier sometimes, most of the time, to just stay where we are. But when we choose to settle in, to stay on the couch, we are stunting our own growth. When a plant starts to outgrow its pot or planter, you have to move it into something bigger, right? Otherwise, its roots will become a tangled mess, and it could die.

Likewise, sometimes it seems like Jesus is asking a lot of us. The next planter looks pretty large. He might ask us to move, to change jobs, to end or start relationships, to talk to strangers, to be vulnerable, to be generous, to love our enemies, to do something that seems to make no sense. We don't feel equipped for many of these things. But we will never grow, and our comfort zone will stay small, if we're never willing to step outside of it. Let Jesus plant you in a bigger pot.

When I was 21, I co-led a group of girls on a mission trip to Peru. And there were definitely moments when I felt like I had bitten off more than I could chew. But, I remember talking to God about it all, telling him I didn't think I was the right woman for this job, when he just popped a little picture into my mind that I'll never forget.

I saw myself as a five-year-old child, standing in my parents' bedroom with my dad's jeans around my ankles. Obviously they were just a *little* too big for me. But the Father simply looked at me and said,

"Put on a belt. You'll grow into them. I've given you everything you need in the meantime."

We aren't going to be a perfect fit right away for everything we ever do. But the Father equips us as we go, and one day you'll look down at your waistline in wonder, seeing that these pants were indeed created just for you. It just took a little time to grow into them.

I don't know what the next yes will be for you, but I encourage you to choose to say yes now, even before Jesus presents the opportunity in great detail. Agree to put on whatever pants he hands you through the dressing room door. He knows you. He isn't going to put you into a pair of hideous lime green bell bottoms just to embarrass you. That's not who he is.

Maybe you've heard about Jesus, but you're a little unsure about all this. Say yes to seeing what he's like.

Maybe you've had a relationship with Jesus for a while, but you've gotten comfortable. Say yes to getting off the couch.

Maybe you're going through a job change or a move or starting college. Maybe you're in a serious relationship. Say yes to going where he leads, even if it's a little scary.

Say yes to dreaming with God; say yes to the possibility of failing. Say yes to taking a step, even when it's scary. Say yes to doing the hard things and the uncomfortable things. Say yes to loving hard and to caring for your neighbors and your friends and your family. Say yes to coffee with the new girl at work who needs a listening ear. Say yes to the second date, even if you aren't positive you're going to marry him. Say yes to locking eyes with God when you're afraid.

I pray that you would just ask Jesus what his next invitation is for you, and that you would choose to say yes to it. His invitation for you will probably not look like mine, or your mom's, or your best friend's.

Just like different plants grow and bloom in different seasons, so also does our life and our walk with God.

Disclaimer: choosing to say yes now does *not* mean that you say yes to every single opportunity that presents itself. Some of those opportunities will not be from God. Some of those opportunities aren't healthy choices. My encouragement is to choose now to say yes in the future when *God* asks you to do anything. It's a choice to trust that his plan is good. It's a choice to believe that God is in control. It's a choice to walk by faith and not by sight.

* * *

In closing, I want to remind you one more time to keep moving forward. To keep running the race. To keep putting one foot in front of the other, one yes at a time. Don't give up when the going gets tough. Don't give up when something unexpected happens. Don't turn back, don't sit down and pout with your arms crossed (for too long, anyway), don't pack up your things and hightail it down the road.

I shared this verse back in chapter one, and I want to end with it, too: "I don't know about you, but I'm running hard for the finish line. I'm giving it everything I've got. No sloppy living for me! I'm staying alert and in top condition. I'm not going to get caught napping, telling everyone else all about it and then missing out myself" (1 Corinthians 9:26–27).

Let's run together, friends. Let's encourage each other and press on towards the finish line, even when our legs want to quit and our sides are cramping. Let's say yes to whatever he asks of us next. Even if it's hard or weird or boring or awkward!

"After this many of his disciples turned back and no longer walked with him. So Jesus said to the twelve, 'Do you want to go away as well?' Simon Peter answered him, 'Lord, to whom shall we go? You have the words of eternal life, and we have believed, and have come to know, that you are the Holy One of God'" (John 6:66–69).

When I leave this place, may I never be the same. May I not forget who Jesus is or what He has done for me. May I keep moving forward, keep following. No turning back. May I keep choosing yes.

p.s.
still choosing yes

Not long after I finished writing this, I encountered another season of battle. One that I'm still fighting. It hasn't been nearly as crippling as my first go-around, but it hasn't exactly been fun.

I tell you this because I want you to know that there isn't a magic formula out there to make life easier or smoother or better. You can do all the things I talked about in these last pages and still encounter dark seasons. You can pray the "right prayers" and do the "right things," and life is still just hard sometimes. It doesn't mean you're doing it wrong. It doesn't mean Jesus has changed or left you. We just live in a broken world, and evil is a toxic poison that impacts all of our lives. But that doesn't mean you should give up, either. That doesn't mean there isn't hope.

I had a hard time going back and reading what I had written after the first round of edits. And do you know why? I felt like a fraud. How could I have just written all of this and be where I currently am?

But that's how I knew it was the enemy talking. The enemy speaks in lies. The enemy wants me to feel like a fraud. The enemy doesn't want me doing Kingdom work. And I don't think it's coincidental that this battle began after I had just finished writing something that I believe will encourage the hearts of other believers.

So I'm here to say—to you and to myself—that I'm still learning to fight the good fight right along with you. I'm still practicing fixing my eyes on Jesus. I'm pushing myself to keep running. I'm preaching to myself on a daily basis. I'm praying for grace and peace and hope. I haven't got it all down perfectly yet. But even on the hard days, I'm *still choosing yes.*

You're not alone, dear reader.

"May the God of hope fill you with all joy and peace in believing, so that by the power of the Holy Spirit you may abound in hope" (Romans 15:13).

Amen.

thank you

A huge thank you to those who cheered me on, read drafts, and asked me how things were going but didn't ask *too* many questions! (Ha!)

Thank you to my parents, Tharen and Chris, for always loving me, supporting me, praying for me, and letting me go when God asks me to go. Thank you for being examples of Jesus to me.

To my siblings, nieces, and nephew: Thank you for your love, friendship, and many laughs. Hope to see you soon.

Thank you Jess, Jessica, and Kelli for your amazing feedback, edits, comments, and text messages on the first drafts of this baby! Jess, you've walked much of this journey with me, and I will be eternally thankful for your friendship. Jessica, thank you for sharing your heart, your wisdom, and your struggles with me. We are in this together! And Kelli, thank you for always voicing your support, for believing in me, and for the daily chats.

Thank you, April, for being my first and the most excited cheerleader a girl could ask for. And it was so fun to write books at the same time. (Everyone, go buy *And If I Don't?* by April Klassen!)

Lauren, David, Hazel, Iris, Mari, and Elias: Thank for your investment and love in my life. For all your prayers, words of affirmation, and encouragement to follow Jesus.

To my forever friends, Brooke and Emma, thank you for being loyal, for letting me pursue my dreams even though we are always too far away, and for *knowing* me.

Carly and Diane, thank you for the excitement you bring to my life, your friendship and encouragement, and sleepovers.

Thank you to my Canadian families—the Sutherlands and the Klassens (the Steve-and-Lisa Klassens!)—for making me feel welcome in Canada, for your investment in my walk with Jesus, and for all the meals and snacks you fed me.

Thank you to my Harmony Heartthrobs, Erin and Joanie, for some of the most memorable moments in Canada. Here's to all the dance parties, ice cream stops, and flower heists.

Thank you to my sweet editor, Angie, for all your help and encouragement!

And thank you to so many more...my team at Multiply, my huddle at ACC, the TREK participants and teachers and staff...I love you all, and you are part of my story.

May we all keep choosing yes.

notes

1. *Stop Trying to "Find Yourself," RightNow Media* (RightNow Ministries, 2017), https://www.rightnowmedia.org/Content/illustration/180344.

2. John Mark Comer, *God Has a Name* (Grand Rapids, MI: Zondervan, 2017), 50-51.

3. Rob Reimer, *Soul Care: 7 Transformational Principles for a Healthy Soul* (Franklin, TN: Carpenter's Son Publishing, 2016), 46.

4. Reimer, *Soul Care*, 66.

5. Kelly Clarkson, "Stronger (What Doesn't Kill You)," Track 2 on *Stronger*, RCA Records, 2011, compact disc.

6. D.W. Ekstrand, "Dying to Self," Dying to Self, 2012, http://www.thetransformedsoul.com/additional-studies/spiritual-life-studies/dying-to-self.

7. Donald Miller, *Blue Like Jazz* (Nashville, TN: Thomas Nelson, 2003), 12.

about the author

Becky Spahr is a lover of laughter, an eater of french-fries, and most importantly, a follower of Jesus. She loves to write, design, create, and teach. Originally from Kansas, she's had the opportunity to serve around the world in various capacities as a Kingdom worker. Her calling in life is to *create* beautiful and useful things, *cultivate* spaces for growth and discipleship, and *celebrate* what the LORD is doing in and around the world.

Manufactured by Amazon.ca
Bolton, ON